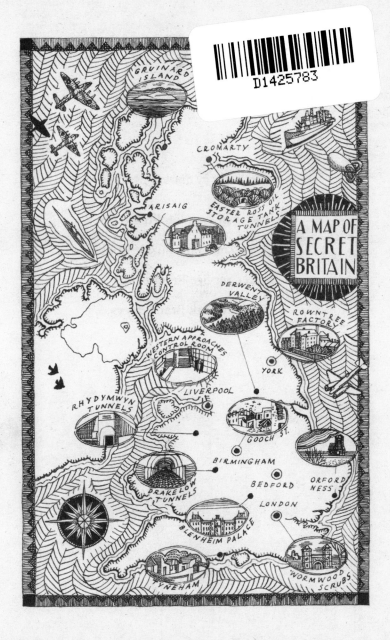

A MAP OF SECRET BRITAIN

GRUINARD ISLAND

CROMARTY

EASTER ROSS OIL STORAGE TANK TUNNELS

ARISAIG

DERWENT VALLEY

ROWNTREE FACTORY

WESTERN APPROACHES CONTROL ROOM

YORK

RHYDYMWYN TUNNELS

LIVERPOOL

GOOCH ST.

BIRMINGHAM

ORFORD NESS

DRAKELOW TUNNELS

BEDFORD

LONDON

BLENHEIM PALACE

TYNEHAM

WORMWOOD SCRUBS

SINCLAIR McKAY

SECRET BRITAIN

A Journey Through the Second World War's
Hidden Bases and Battlegrounds

HEADLINE

First published in 2021 by
HEADLINE PUBLISHING GROUP

First published in paperback in 2022 by
HEADLINE PUBLISHING GROUP

1

Please refer to page 300 for picture credits.
Illustration on page i © Helen Cann 2021

Cataloguing in Publication Data is available from the British Library

ISBN 978 1 4722 8455 6

Designed and typeset by EM&EN
Printed and bound in Great Britain by Clays Ltd, Elcograf S.p.A.

HEADLINE PUBLISHING GROUP
An Hachette UK Company
Carmelite House
50 Victoria Embankment
London EC4Y 0DZ

www.headline.co.uk
www.hachette.co.uk

Contents

Introduction

If you take a bracing walk along the clifftops of Dorset, looking out at the vast expanse of blue sea, on one stretch of the path you might see an elegant abstract sculpture on a plinth. It is made up of intertwining bands of gold, suggestive of a radar dish. On this spot, in the summer of 1940, scientists perfected a miracle to help save the nation from invasion. Elsewhere, in quiet Bedfordshire, there is a gravely dignified stately home, which, from 1939, played host to a brilliant crowd of young women who were engaged in life-or-death work which had consequences right the way across the world. On a trip to London, a ramble through a slightly rackety 1930s-built suburb near Wembley will bring you within view of a large institutional-looking redbrick building which rarely merits a second glance. And yet it was here, in the twilight of the Second World War, that the future age of computers was forged by a handful of people who barely comprehended the full epoch-changing significance of what was happening.

What these – and a huge number of other sites dotted up and down the length of the UK – have in common was that they were once places of top secrecy. From busy research stations to laboratories where boffins set about trying to create 'death rays', there were super-restricted clandestine houses and huts and stretches of open moorland that were strictly forbidden for the general public. There were bases from which vast battles were directed, institutions where astounding espionage gadgets and explosive sabotage equipment were perfected and tested and stretches of beautiful wilderness that became roaring battlegrounds, where deadly serious rehearsals for war were played out. There were corners of the country where the curious were not even allowed a glimpse. But now the public *is* allowed. And there is an entire country of secrets to be explored.

For quite a long time, eerie inner-city bombsites and derelict airfields covered with weeds and rubble were the chief landmarks of Britain's war years. Haunting visual reminders of ordeal and heroism: however, thanks to the gradual relaxation of the Official Secrets Act in specific historic cases, there are now many other kinds of war landmarks – some hugely uplifting and quirky and celebratory – that are now accessible and open. For a long time, some were overlooked altogether; most of us wouldn't have known they had played a part in the conflict at all.

For instance, few would have thought much of the entrance of an old disused London underground station in Mayfair – yet it was here where Churchill used to come at night to visit the secret subterranean operations base for the nation's railways. He also came in order to have some thinking time away from the War Rooms, and to avail himself of a splendidly large bathtub to be found in a side tunnel. Equally, walkers in the Mendip Hills today would scarcely register the concrete remains of a small hill-top bunker dug into the earth and yet it was from here that improbably, on the darkest nights, German bombers above were tricked and dazzled with pyrotechnic effects.

Even familiar landmarks, such as the splendour of Blenheim Palace in Oxfordshire and the stern and austere Wormwood Scrubs prison in west London, have layers of hidden wartime history echoing within their walls. In both these cases, it was the intrigue and ingenuity of espionage. But in all of these instances, the paramount need for secrecy obscured all. Nor did anyone quite know when this secrecy should stop. And so, it was only in more recent years that large numbers of these brilliant Second World War sites began to reveal their extraordinary stories.

Secrecy was something that the British public turned out to have a terrific talent for (unlike their American counterparts, who were as leaky as colanders when it came to hush-hush matters). When war came on 3 September 1939, one of the government's first moves was to alert the public to the idea that there could be undercover Nazi spies moving among them, in every town, every village, every office and every pub and cinema. Ministers got to work on the propaganda that would ensure caution. They commissioned a series of posters with cartoons painted by artist Cyril Bird that were witty and effective. They depicted men and women either in the saloon bar, or in trains, or in factories, all crowding in for chinwags about their war work. And the tagline was always the same: 'Careless Talk Costs Lives'. The government launched what it termed an 'anti-gossip' campaign. The aim was to inform the working population that any scrap of information shared could give a German spy a great advantage in the war. And it worked: the British were swiftly trained into the habit of super-secrecy.

In 1939, this veil of discretion was lowered over the railways and the roads too. Platform station-names were removed and signposts were taken down. The aim was to disorientate possible German infiltrators and the fact that it also confused everyone else was neither here nor there. For the point was that the population broadly approved of this new approach to life; it made people feel they were making a palpable contribution to the war effort.

And more than that, for the many thousands of young people recruited into secret work – from radio interception and scientific research to the hiding of priceless works of art – there was also an intense pride. When they went home on leave and when family and friends badgered them for clues about what they were doing, they could reply with some dignity that they were sworn to secrecy by the Crown. Indeed, for the small army of teenage radio fanatics recruited to help harvest German messages, this was every bit as good as the fictional espionage sagas that they devoured at the time.

It wasn't just roads and railways; entire swathes of the British landscape also became top secret. Stately homes deep in the countryside were requisitioned and turned to a wide range of hidden purposes, as the villagers round and about fruitlessly tried to guess. Meanwhile, beneath the streets of major cities, old brick tunnel systems were extended and given a variety of amazing uses, from factories to intelligence nerve centres.

And now, decades later, the landscape of Secret Britain is emerging from the shadows. We can go on a journey to visit the lonely coastal laboratories, the remote moorland turned into combat training grounds, the estuary where rocket experiments were carried out and the strange earthworks burrowed beneath forests, some of which are still only just being uncovered, and which are found to still contain bedding and tins. There's a whole world of Second World War history out there ready to be explored.

A few of these formerly secret sites have recently been basking in fame having received belated tribute. Bletchley Park in Buckinghamshire is the most lustrous example. In the grounds of this slightly drab Victorian country house was arguably one of the greatest secrets of the Second World War, a codebreaking operation so brilliantly successful that on a daily basis its intelligence was helping to change the course of the conflict. In and around the estate worked young women and men, from mathematicians to poets to Wrens who were cryptic crossword enthusiasts. All signed the Official Secrets Act. All were required to say not one word about what they had done – in theory, for the rest of their lives. Thankfully, we are now able to tell their stories and commemorate their incredible ingenuity and achievements.

The story of Secret Britain is in part a celebration. There are tales of brilliant inventiveness and beguiling quirkiness to be told, from a boffin in a secret hut jumping out of his skin as a bullet from an enemy aircraft ricocheted around his metal filing cabinet, to the women in a secret bunker who were ceremonially hoisted up and turned upside down so that they could plant their footsteps on the ceiling as initiation. There are stories of the most intense endeavour, where young women in hidden underground bunkers intently listened through the night to decipher messages from enemy ships knowing that one tiny mistake could bring disaster and death. Elsewhere, ordinary people were being trained in country houses to become saboteurs and killers – and sometimes being ordered to drink vast quantities of alcohol to monitor how they would keep their heads if entrapped in enemy honey-traps.

But this wartime story also makes us look at the land itself with fresh eyes too. In a time when we have all been emerging from restricted lives and discovering a new and keener appetite to explore corners of the country that had been forbidden by lockdown, there are extra reasons to relish the rich layers of the past. Now we have the renewed freedom to do so, this is a wonderful time to set out and enjoy – for instance – the silvery dunes of the storm-blown north Devon coast, where secret rehearsals for D-Day were carried out. Or to immerse ourselves in the soft emerald and chalk undulations of Dorset, where a beautiful hamlet was sacrificed for vital training manoeuvres. Or to join tours to investigate the ghostly abandoned London Underground stations that can still, just about, be glimpsed from the windows of today's trains.

This is a story of how even in a landscape that is timelessly exquisite, history has many more surprises to yield up, making us appreciate it all the more.

SECRET WILDERNESSES

The Dark Highlands

Arisaig, Inverness-shire

The men and women who were brought here were being taught to kill. Yet even the most hardened recruits must have been struck by the almost other-worldly beauty of these training grounds. The gentle fir-bristling slopes rising in the distance towards mountains that filled the sky, the fresh, rippling cold waters of the loch, reflected glittering blue under sunshine and the salt air carrying news of the wider oceans beyond. Then there was the house. A large manor with ash-granite dignity, its thick walls suggestive of protection and warmth. But for the young recruits to the Special Operations Executive, the life that lay ahead held very little prospect of comfort. And their deadly rehearsals here were easy to keep a secret, for this was one of the least populated areas of the British Isles. That remains the case today, except for the hardy visitors and intrigued tourists.

Arisaig is in the north-west of Scotland, a grassy peninsula before the dreamier prospect of Skye and the Hebrides. It was to this place that the extraordinarily courageous agents of the Special Operations Executive –

Churchill's 'Ministry of Ungentlemanly Warfare' – were brought by rail from Glasgow's Buchanan Street. The line lazily follows the edges of Loch Lomond before pushing into the wilder lands beyond.

And Arisaig House was where trainee secret agents were taught the final flourishes of sabotage and self-defence – from the arts of explosives to the fine-tuning of Morse code and telegraphy, to effective camouflage. The Special Operations Executive had been commissioned to 'set Europe ablaze'[1] through subversion and direct action. But their reach spread further into Africa, and on to the Far East. These women and men, operating far from any notion of safety or sanctuary and often alone or with clandestine local resistance, were sabotaging railway lines and planting explosives ingeniously disguised as potatoes. They also were transmitting intelligence from radios cunningly designed to resemble logs and branches. To be caught was to face torture and – very often – death. All recruits knew the hideous risks. Arisaig was where they were tutored in endurance and the wiles to evade the enemy's lethal clutches. Dodging across this rugged countryside were recruits such as Virginia Hall (who had a prosthetic leg after having accidentally shot herself in the foot a few years earlier), an eastern European aristocrat called Krystyna Skarbek (described by pioneering SOE spymaster Vera Atkins as 'very brave, very attractive, but a law unto herself'[2]) and a man who was to serve as part-inspiration for Ian Fleming's James Bond, the writer Patrick Leigh-Fermor.

Isolated beauty: Loch nan Uamh, Arisaig.

For some SOE agents, this corner of Scotland marked the turning point in the way that they would see the world for the rest of their lives. Recruits such as Harry Ree, a young schoolmaster from Lancashire, went from here out to a world that was vivid and terrifying, filled with the starkest reality about betrayal and faithfulness and human morality. Arisaig was a portal – not only elemental and raw in terms of landscape but leading to a landscape of war in which the most ordinary people could either be monsters or saints. To train among these wilds was to be given just the most fleeting taste of true, frightening human vulnerability and isolation, for once these secret operatives were then parachuted into France,

Greece and elsewhere into the darkest regions of the war, all they were left with were their wits and self-reliance.

Some of the female recruits to SOE were later to be justly celebrated for their incredible bravery and sacrifice. Women such as Violette Szabo and the above-mentioned Virginia Hall and Krystyna Skarbek are inspirational to this day. But before they were sent into Nazi-occupied Europe to fulfil their missions (of which we will read more shortly), they passed through Arisaig House.

If you received the tap on the shoulder as a possible recruit to SOE, there was a short course of initial training at Wanborough, an Elizabethan house in Surrey. As well as the expected cross-country dashes and map-reading tests, there were more unexpected challenges, including drinking ordeals. How much booze could a candidate imbibe while still keeping a level analytical head and a firmly closed mouth? Those who passed the aptitude tests then boarded those north-facing trains to a house that was wreathed in a Scottish mist of obscurity. Just a couple of stops before the end of the line – and the open sea – at Mallaig, the recruits entered a new and much more dangerous world. Here they would be expected to not merely survive, but to succeed.

Indeed, even before they left that unheated train, there was every chance that they would have found themselves under attack. Trainee agents already at Arisaig were sometimes ordered to hijack the Fort William to Mallaig service as essential exercises.

One of the arms instructors at Arisaig who tutored

these new young people in the subtleties of gunplay was Gavin Maxwell, who would later become celebrated for his much-loved 1960 nature book *Ring of Bright Water*, involving wild otters raised as pets. Here, amid the richness of the natural world that he loved, he was imparting the knowledge on the sharpest and fastest ways to kill.

There were more silent means of vanquishing the enemy. Two veterans of the Shanghai Police were at Arisaig to teach the most effective means of prevailing in knife fights. William Fairburn and Bill Sykes, who in previous incarnations had fought the bloodthirsty criminal gangs of Shanghai, went so far as to jointly develop what they considered the *ne plus ultra* of fighting daggers. It was amid the scented pines and firs surrounding the house that their flesh-slicing technique was taught. While regular soldiers had the closeness of comradeship, these agents had to establish their own moral certainties and establish complete independence.

Arisaig House, built in 1863, had been requisitioned from its smart owner almost as soon as war was declared in September 1939. This property – and many others located across the Highlands – ushered in not just British recruits, but Poles and Czech agents too. They were eventually to be infiltrated deep into hostile territory across Europe, into landscapes that were fiercer and wilder than the Scottish land they trained on. Here at Arisaig they would learn to negotiate mountains with complex equipment, guns and explosives, and since the surrounding area was under Special Protection, not even the Highland locals knew truly what any of them were up to. The agents-to-be were billeted not at the house itself, but in smaller properties close by. A hut within the grounds of Arisaig was used not for accommodation, but for terrifying interrogations. A purpose-built cell to give the spies a taste of what would happen if they were captured, and to try to impart rudimentary means of resisting giving out any intelligence.

Compared to the reality of what the Gestapo could offer – not merely in terms of inflicting agony but in using that publicly paraded agony to then put pressure on suspected associates – training could only ever impart a forewarning of the horrific reality. But to have got this far within the entire induction, the recruits had proved their implacable determination.

Sometimes these women and men were recruited because of their heritage and their dexterity with languages. Sometimes it was because it was clear that their extreme zeal to defeat the Nazis would have been wasted in passive roles in aeroplane factories. Violette Szabo was such an example. Born in Paris in 1921 to a French mother and English father, she came to live in London in 1932. As war broke out, she was working in a department store in the unglamorous district of Brixton. It was after the war broke out that she met her husband to be, Etienne Szabo. Their courtship was a whirlwind; marriage was swift, and so too was the tragedy brought by the tempest of war. He was killed in north Africa, leaving Violette with a baby daughter.

A portrait of courage: British–French Special Operations Executive agent Violette Reine Elizabeth Szabo.

Rather than succumbing to grief, Violette was instead seized by the compulsion to avenge him. By this stage working at a plant in Morden, south London, her effortless bilingualism was noted. Following an interview with the recruiter (and novelist) Selywn Gypson, she was inducted into training.

Women were expected to endure as much physical hardship as the men at Arisaig – the all-night manoeuvres on the freezing moonlit hills, and the exacting tutorials on the use of everything from pistols to machine guns to high explosives. There were also more specialised skills to be learned such as the correct way to blow up railway lines (these laid for purpose, not the ones running to Mallaig, thankfully). In the case of Szabo, who was twice parachuted into Nazi occupied France to organise sabotage and to work with the Maquis (the rural bands of French resistance fighters), Arisaig was a sort of university of the espionage dark arts. In amid all the other paramilitary training, she was also a brilliant markswoman. Indeed, she was reckoned to have been one of the very best shots to have trained at Arisaig. On her second mission into the field, Szabo's exceptional courage led her into an extraordinary gun battle in a field with German troops. As it intensified, she was providing cover for fleeing Maquisards but in the end, because of an earlier injury to her ankle, she could not escape herself. She was captured and withstood brutal torture. She was transferred to Ravensbruck concentration camp where she continued to defy her sociopathic captors, but cruelly in the end she was executed. Her daughter Tania, who had been billeted with childminders, would in 1946 be invited as a four-year-old to Buckingham Palace to receive her mother's posthumous George Cross from King George VI.

Another female agent, the Polish countess Krsytyna Skarbek (who adopted the alias Christine Grenville while escaping Nazi-occupied Hungary and then kept the name thereafter) was hugely enthusiastic about parachute jumping and extreme skiing, and she was luckier in her terrifying wartime exploits deep in France (working under moonlight to ensure smuggled arms got to the Resistance) and on sabotage and subversion operations in the Alps. She had returned from earlier missions into central Europe and north Africa with microfilms proving that Hitler was poised to invade the Soviet Union. But she was treated abominably after the war; the authorities declared they had no further use for her and did not see why she shouldn't be deported to the now Soviet Poland. This would have meant her having to face Stalin's death squads. She escaped that fate but was later to be murdered by an unhinged lover in the foyer of a London hotel.

One of the more extraordinary undercover episodes of the war was in part made possible by Arisaig. Arriving at the estate in the winter of 1941 were a handful of exiled Czech soldiers. Two in particular, Jozef Gabcik and Jan Kubis, were selected for a high-profile assassination mission. Their target: the Nazi Reinhard Heydrich, also known as the 'Butcher of Prague'[3] and the Protector of Bohemia and Moravia. In the spring of 1942, having been infiltrated into Czechoslovakia, the assassins targeted Heydrich in his open-topped car. The resulting explosion caused 'the Butcher' agonising injuries and a lingering death. But the Nazi reprisals, involving thousands of arrests and murders of suspected dissidents, were appalling. The two agents themselves, with a group of Czech comrades, were soon hunted down, and both died after a vicious gun battle in a Prague cathedral.

Then there were agents like Harry Ree, who survived his war, and who returned thereafter to his first love of teaching. His school was a comprehensive in a deeply deprived area of north-east London. Throughout his time working with factions of the French resistance – successfully destroying factories, blocking a busy working canal with a hijacked vehicle, and carrying out many other acts of sabotage besides – he had formed many close friendships with people whom he remembered as being exceptional for their very ordinariness. This was not a war where heroes fitted an archetype. The genuine heroes, with illimitable courage and fortitude, were the women and men who would never usually have received a second glance and who were certainly not extroverted.

Arisaig was not the only Highlands secret site. Nearby, SOE had commandeered houses such as Rhubana Lodge, Inverailort Castle (the SOE's first site) and, in the Cairngorms to the east, an estate called Drumintoul. This was chosen for a highly specific reason: training SOE agents to operate in the freezing whiteness of Norway. Here amid these high mountains was a landscape every bit as sharp and icy and unyielding as the one that the agents were going to face in the field. And these agents would be on one of the defining missions of the war: sabotaging Nazi progress towards the atomic bomb by raiding a Norwegian heavy water plant called Vemork. 'Heavy water' was an engineered liquid designed to slow down neutrons and it created a means whereby uranium could be transformed to plutonium, one of the crucial materials for creating atomic blasts.

Many of the agents were Norwegians who had succeeded in escaping the Nazi invasion to form a resistance. Though they passed through Arisaig, these agents learned the craft of handling explosives more thoroughly amid the snowy moors of Drumintoul. The base helped sharpen their cross-country skiing skills, which were needed to get away from the pursuing enemy once the heavy water plant had been comprehensively destroyed.

Despite the intense secrecy that was cloaked over Arisaig throughout the war, its history has been quietly marked. The village itself now has a memorial specifically for the Czech and Slovak soldiers who were trained there. A half-opened parachute in grey granite gives way to honoured names, and the code-terms for their missions. In addition, a local museum bears exhibits and photographs from a time when Arisaig's children must have been completely agog with curiosity about all the activity around the large handsome house, screened with vast rhododendrons.

And the house itself wears its legacy lightly: its latest incarnation (although it is currently up for sale) was as a smart and relaxed hotel, a symphony of tartan and leather armchairs. The sort of creature comforts that those 3,000 courageous SOE trainee agents that passed through here would have sighed for.

HOW TO GET THERE

Arisiaig lies on the A830. The nearest big town, Fort William, is about an hour's drive away. Though it might be worth bearing in mind that the train journey, involving moors and mountains and lochs and viaducts, is beautiful. Arisaig station is roughly five hours' journey from Glasgow Queen Street.

The Rockets in the Dunes

Ynyslas, near Borth, Dyfed

These vast sand dunes, a maze with twisting hollows, lie between the silver sea and the rich green hills of the wide Dyfi estuary. This is the very centre of the coastline of Wales. Look north and you will see the distant mountains. The sand dunes themselves are consistently restless with the wind and the crying birds, and yet they are also a sanctuary of peace. This was not always the case. One might imagine that it would be rather difficult to keep war research involving roaring rockets a secret. Yet in 1945, towards the end of the war, the dunes of Ynyslas played host to a most remarkable convocation of scientific minds and eager volunteer ATS (Auxiliary Territorial Service) women. Extraordinarily – thanks to obliging locals in the nearby coastal village of Borth – their research remained confidential and indeed had a bearing on post-war rocket work.

'The sea and the estuary were used for testing different types of firing shells,' recalled ATS volunteer Margaret Herterich years later. 'The girls, smartly dressed in black reefer jackets and berets, were placed at different obser-

A real blast: out on the shore with Women's ATS personnel.

vation posts around the area where we read off bearings and information from our equipment.'[4] Occasionally, the reward for this very precise confidential work in sometimes wild conditions was an immensely civilised tea on board a naval craft moored in the Estuary. Yet there was nothing remotely whimsical about the task in hand.

One of the aims of the rocket scientists of Ynyslas was to find a means of countering and matching Hitler's 'Vengeance' or V-weapons: the lethal missile and rockets that, from the summer of 1944, began falling from the sky and bringing death without warning to busy streets and terraces in the Home Counties. While the Nazis had dedicated rocket technology obsessives like the aristocratic scientist Werner von Braun, the British, though not as advanced, were also exploring the possibilities of sending weapons high into the stratosphere. Sir Alwyn D. Crow, the Director of Guided Projectiles at the Ministry of Supply, was the mastermind who sought to bring other experts to a brand-new secret launching site in the west of Wales.

Those who received the summons included scientists from Frank Whittle's Power Jets (Research and Development) and Laporte Chemicals, as well as fuel companies and radar departments (to track the progress of the test rockets). In all, there were some forty scientists and around 200 ATS women. In amid the wide dunes and grassy hummocks that ran from the beach and stretched inland along the reedy estuary, there were specially constructed launching ramps and towers. It was a mini Cape Kennedy, utilitarian but at the same time surrounded by lush beauty.

And this was one of the more congenial secret sites of the war. Operating towards the end of the conflict, those who worked there must have had their minds already fixed on the world that was to come after victory. In addition to this, there is something about this landscape even in the winter that causes the heart to skitter a little with enthusiasm for life, especially when the westward skies form steel grey curtains that bring biblical rainstorms to the yellow sands.

Despite the relative remoteness, this part of Wales was by no means distant from the war. Right from the start, the nearby seaside holiday town of Aberystwyth had been playing host to a variety of evacuated students from the University of London, who themselves were graduating to the war effort. One such English Literature scholar, Mavis Batey, was drawn into the gravitational pull of Bletchley Park (see 'An Asylum for Geniuses', p.201). A few miles down the coast from this stood the airstrips of RAF Aberporth, which had – on top of its other military responsibilities – seen a variety of airborne experiments and some missile launches of its own. Cardigan Bay, further south, also saw a huge amount of weapons testing. The nature of the new technology of rockets, however, meant that a heavier burden of total secrecy lay over Ynysglas. The experiments were the precursors to grander post-war scientific endeavours, in particular the efforts to develop a rocket system known as Blue Streak.

The top-secret Ynysglas rocket range lay some distance off the main road between Aberystwyth and inland Machynlleth, yet for the scientists and the ATS women, escape was also possible by railway from Borth station, further up the dunes. A little over two hours on the train and they could be in Birmingham. The location meant that rockets could also be brought in and kept aboard ships that floated in the wide estuary of the River Dyfi. Also useful, in terms of rocket landings, were the vast mudflats that lay between Ynysglas and the northerly coastline.

The local people would be largely left to guess at the nature of the work hidden behind the barbed-wire enclosures around the dunes. This part of Wales –

Welsh-speaking, largely rural – was phlegmatic about the distant roars and booms. Indeed, in the wilder winter nights, when storms raged in across the sea, the sounds of war and the boom of nature might have been difficult to distinguish.

The facilities at Ynysglas were as sparse as the open landscape: brick-built huts, and the use of an old house lying a little way from the beach. Some other houses close by were used to billet some staff. The wider area became home to some enthusiastic newcomers. Sidney Arthur, who hailed from London's East End, and who had worked at the Dagenham Car Works before the war, had been pulled into munitions. Eventually, he and his family including their young daughter Colleen, moved to Borth. The little girl knew nothing of what was happening at Ynysglas, apart from a curious clue that came on VE Day in 1945 when there was a sudden a series of startlingly loud pops and explosions from the direction of the sand dunes.

Several women were there to carry out tests by capturing the flights of rockets on film: this was so that they could be more closely studied. Margaret Herterich recalled the need for her to develop expertise not only as a scientific cinemaphotographer, but also with the maddening mathematics of weighting the huge cameras with ropes and pulleys to better follow the trajectories of fired missiles. This was a world in which the finest calculations of trigonometry had to be conducted in frequently unforgiving weather conditions. Projectiles were

The secret of sands: the beautiful submerged forest of Borth at low tide.

fired, their courses filmed as far as was possible. The film was then taken to an on-camp darkroom (more brick and concrete huts) and the results then studied by platoons of pipe-smoking officers and scientists. At the end of it all, when the war was over and advanced rocket technology needed even more room for testing, some of the young women were thrilled to be asked if they would like to continue their work right the way across the world under the more dependable sunshine of Woomera in Australia.

And the dunes themselves are now a rightly celebrated site, teeming with wildlife and the fascinating echoes of natural history. There are larks in the blowy skies above and out in the far waves, dolphins and porpoises are often seen. The dunes and the saltmarshes around are rich in rare insects, wildflowers and orchids. Nesting deep in those gulleys of sand can be found birds such as stonechats, linnets and plovers. There is also a haunted remnant of centuries-old forest claimed by the sea and at low tide, the exposed tree trunks become visible from beneath the salt water. Meanwhile, the nearby village of Borth is a brightly painted prospect of sturdy nineteenth-century houses facing out over silken beaches. It is easy to imagine that if you were to be posted anywhere during the war, Borth must have seemed an unusually uplifting prospect, not least because the utilitarian base, concrete walls and bare brick huts were overwhelmed by the sheer force of natural beauty all around.

HOW TO GET THERE

The drive across the heart of Wales, while picturesque, is also quite twisty and turny. If possible, the train that runs from Shrewsbury to Aberstwyth is the more relaxing option, and the journey through the rich countryside of Machynlleth, opening out on to the Dyfi estuary, is especially hypnotic. Ynyslas can be reached via bus from Aberystwyth or Borth (Mid Wales Travel 512).

Rehearsals for a Bomber's Moon

Derwent Valley, Derbyshire and South Yorkshire

The perspex was filtered blue and the goggles were amber. During the day, this was the most effective means of turning the sky dark and simulating moonlight. To fly low at great speeds across these bleak prehistoric moors, and then along the vast man-made courses of water, to the incongruously gothic towers marking the point where the water was held back, could hardly be kept a secret from the farmers and villagers who lived nearby. But they could not begin to speculate what, in 1943, the RAF was planning and why the huge reservoirs of the Derwent Valley were buzzing with so much noise. Top secrecy was vital. These RAF crews were not training for the bombing of German cities, but the specific targeting of gigantic dams in the Ruhr.

It is very far from being a secret now, of course. Indeed, immediately after the raid, all was known – and the 1955 film *The Dam Busters* ensured a full uncovering of the clandestine rehearsals 617 Squadron performed in the Derwent Valley. The film, starring Richard Todd, tells the story of their astounding feat and courage and was made partly on location in Durham. Nonetheless, in the twilight of the conflict, the well-established national habit of not asking questions was very much the case here, even as farmers sourly observed that the low-flying Lancasters were causing their cows to dry up with sheer fright.

Derwent and Howden dams, close to the city of Sheffield and high up near Dark Peak, lay in a twisting and turning valley that resembled the target in Germany. The slopes rising from the water bristled with fir trees and heather, and the higher spaces gave way to the rich peaty bogs of the moors. The area was sparsely populated. In fact, the coming of these reservoirs at the turn of the century had depleted the local population. In order for the Victorian engineers to create this large expanse of fresh water, the village of Derwent had to be sacrificed. Its cottages, eighteenth-century manor house and church were all drowned and the villagers were moved out to towns nearby. But the ghosts of their old homes sometimes make themselves known. When water levels drop, the ruined church spire and even some roofs can be glimpsed in those dark depths.

Those who remained in the area had already seen the horrors of the aerial war. German bombers lethally targeted Sheffield in December 1940 over the course of four nights, making that city of molten steel glow gold through the night. Later, on the surrounding hills, decoy lights and fires were deployed (as we shall see later) in efforts to confuse the German bomb aimers. But it was a source of some vexation in 1943 when the people of

Re-staging history: Upper Derwent Valley with two Lancaster bombers passing the Derwent Dam.

the moors found their skies rumbling with what to them seemed like clapped out Lancasters. These runs through the Derwent Valley were not just held during the day but – as proficiency increased – so the rehearsals were carried over into the deep nights. It was said that roof tiles were loosened by the pulsating vibrations.

If they could have known what was being tested here, those villagers might have felt a thrill of local pride. Barnes Wallis was a Derbyshire man and it was his extraordinary creation that was to be deployed against those German dams. The idea for the 'bouncing bomb' – a revolutionary projectile calibrated to hit the water and rise again, spinning until it had hit the stone base of the vast dam walls – was formulated when Barnes Wallis studied the physics of marbles bouncing on the surface of a small pool in his back garden. Bomber Command had long been targeting German factories and synthetic oil plants and it was thought that if the Mohne, Eder and Sorpe dams could be shattered, then the resulting flooding of the industrialised Ruhr valley areas, key centres of war production, that lay below would be catastrophic.

The developed bombs were in fact drum-shaped, rather than balls. And they had to be deployed in the most agonisingly precise way. They had to be dropped on water from a height of sixty feet – extraordinarily low for a bomber – and at a speed of 232 miles per hour. As soon as the bomb hit the water, it would spin backwards as it hurtled towards the stone of the dam.

And so, 617 Squadron was assembled, under Wing Commander Guy Gibson, who was only twenty-four years old. His crews hailed not only from Britain, but also America, Australia, New Zealand and Canada. Because the story of what they achieved has become incredibly familiar over the decades that have passed since, it is easy to take for granted the fact that it was not merely a technical triumph, but also a testament of true bravery. The lives of bomber crews were exceptionally fragile. By 1943, there had been tens of thousands of losses, where young men plummeted from flaming planes into the darkness. Back at base, those who survived could see the empty beds; the slender chances of survival were no secret. Yet they were all volunteers. This was courage that had a metaphysical dimension. Many of these volunteers were addicted to flying and despite death reaching out to them on every mission those moments high in the moonlit sky filled them with wonder.

The men who undertook the secret training missions following the silver course of the Derwent waters were no different, but what they were training for was, for a time, a complete mystery. Guy Gibson was initially the only one who knew the true purpose of the mission – the secrecy was that intense. One of the crew members recalled that even when they used the mock-gothic towers on either side of the Derwent Reservoir wall as markers, they were still not told what their ultimate goal was. They only knew it required training and bravery by the bucket load. Strikingly, it was not only the local cows who were disturbed by the plane's proximity to earth and water: even though one bomb aimer had been on flights

Wing Commander Guy Gibson VC, Commanding Officer of 617 Squadron.

in Lincolnshire where pilots had narrowly whooshed over bridges, or underneath electricity cables, this for him was a new level of risk altogether. After some training flights, he recalled, the plane was found to have bits of branch and twigs sticking to its wings.

The role of the bomb aimers was, naturally, beyond painstaking. There were endless runs of trial and error with dummy bombs in an age before any kind of computer aid. It was a hyper-focused matter of lining sights up, combined with an instinct for trigonometry. There were daytime runs in the long cleft between those Derbyshire hills and they would don night-vision goggles to simulate the silvery light of a clear night. Flying just sixty feet over the reservoir and through the valley caused an unexpected and unwelcome side effect: serious bouts of air sickness caused by the bumpy turbulence. There were worse possible consequences, though, including the danger of miscalculation that might bring the plane too close to the surface of the water, which could have ended lethally. This problem was overcome with a system of Aldis Lamps in the front of the plane, casting illumination on the waters below and indicating geometrically the height to maintain. Soon came the point when the bombs – about the height of a man – and the plan for them, was revealed to the crews. From 9.28 p.m. on 16 May 1943, nineteen Lancasters soared into the night in several waves and towards the darkness of Germany. For those 133 crew members, the apprehension – for the mortality rate of bombers blasted out of the sky was huge – must have been beyond intense. As it was, fifty-three of those crew-men were to die that night, and three, having survived their planes being destroyed under fire, were taken prisoner as they parachuted down. But despite the terrifying odds, the other bombers made it through. The first wave punctured the Mohne and Eder dams after midnight, the vast dark waters of the reservoirs gushing with the roar of a tempest through collapsed masonry, and the subsequent waves of bombers attacked the Sorpe, which remained intact. But 1,300 people in those valleys were killed by the flooding and the carnage it caused.

Today, the landscape around Derwent Water attracts historically-minded ramblers, and previous anniversaries of Operation Chastise – which although Gibson and his men pulled it off quite brilliantly, was only debatably successful, since the Ruhr industrial production was only temporarily halted – have been marked by Lancasters leaving their dignified retirement to fly low once more over those steel-grey waters. Of all the secret landscapes, this one was never sealed off with the fences and barbed wire of high-security establishments.

How to get there

There is an Upper Derwent Visitor Centre, from which you can set out on walks to the spectacular dams and on to the hills around. The nearest railway station, some several miles to the south, is Bamford, which has connections to Sheffield and Manchester.

The Fires and the Tombs

Black Down, Mendip Hills, Somerset

There is something curiously atavistic about the image of a fire burning on top of a hill with the sky darkening behind. In centuries past beacons were lit either to celebrate spiritually significant dates, or to guide weary warriors and travellers. In the Second World War, the hill-top fire became reversed in meaning; it was there to deceive and to draw enemies away from their real targets.

The Starfish programme was a nationwide effort to lure the bombers of the Luftwaffe away from their intended industrial city targets. However, the term 'fire' doesn't quite cover it. Up and down the land, north to south, there were brilliant and wonderful gimmicks deployed to make the bombers above think that they were looking down upon actual streets, as opposed to rough dark moorland. (Indeed, in Germany, towns and cities that were being attacked by the RAF used similar strategies). But in England, there was one particular site that seemed suffused with its own extraordinary history and atmosphere, and not just because it lay above the tombs of ancient warriors. The complex and proud pyrotechnics that were staged on

Black Down, a hill-top moor in the Mendips, Somerset, a few miles south of Bristol, were startlingly clever and uniquely eerie.

Those long buried warriors would probably have admired the ingenuity of the living. Starfish employed layers of intricacy and ingenuity to simulate the illusion of factories and trams, and of railways and steelworks. And the man who led the way by inventing ways of making different sorts of light and fire look like railway crossing gates, or even the 'explosion' of a dropped bomb, was Colonel John Turner.

The Colonel was an engineer by training. Already in his early sixties by the outbreak of the war, he had rich experience. His career had begun in 1900 in the Corps of Royal Engineers. When the RAF was fully formed in the aftermath of the First World War, he gave his services as a civil engineer. He also became a fully qualified pilot. By the 1930s, he was Director of Works and Buildings at the Air Ministry. As such, when it came to the top-secret business of defending British cities from the Blitz, here was a figure who combined his practical knowledge with a zesty inventiveness. The luminous innovations that he brought to a number of clandestine sites were both beguilingly simple in principle and yet brilliant in their economical ingenuity.

All Starfish sites were strictly forbidden to the wider public as their very existence was a grave secret. For they were, after all, intended to save countless lives. There were different categories to the deception; some sites were fake airfields, with fake runways and fake aeroplanes, a target for daylight Luftwaffe pilots. Other sites were even more involved and the installation on Black Down was among the most complex. In order to manufacture its full range of trickery, Colonel Turner and his team had requisitioned a corner of Shepperton Film Studios in Surrey. Here, using the expertise of theatrical lighting designers and gifted props men, the plan was to create the impression of a busy city that when seen from hundreds of feet above, would instantly convince the Luftwaffe bombers.

Black Down, high in the Mendips, was (is) a wind-scoured landscape looking out over the distant vista of the Bristol Channel, the Quantock Hills and, to its north, the once-smoky haze of industrial and maritime Bristol. Here near a lonely track, a bunker was built into the earth. It was reasonably elaborate, if small: at one end, there was a generator room, at the other, an operations room. There was electrical wiring and cabling and ventilation. There were also little human touches for the operatives who would be manning this bunker night after night including a small stove, table and chairs. There were also blast walls, air vents and a turret for observation.

And it was from here that the grand illusion was conducted upon receiving news of an imminent bombing raid. Deep under the star-speckled silence of the night sky, the generator would hum into life and the spectacle would begin. With the help of Shepperton lighting technicians, there were illuminations that could flash at intervals, simulating the intensity of arc-welding; there were softer lights, artfully placed in frames, that were there to conjure the impression of a house where someone had forgotten to black-out the windows. There was a deep ruby glow set within a metal box that would look, from above, like the intense coal fire of a steam engine. All of these simulations were co-ordinated and conducted electrically from within that blast-proof bunker.

But even more than this, there were special effects that could cause confusion even if a first wave of bombers had hit their precise targets in Bristol. Colonel Turner and his team gave great thought to what was called the Starfish Boiler. This was a magically simple but brilliant idea. There were two high scaffold towers. On top of one was a tank containing water and on top of the other a tank containing oil. From these were cistern pipes that sloped down to – and converged on – a long central trough. Inside this trough was an electric device primed to ignite. During a bombing raid, oil would be released into the trough, set alight – and then, at intervals, water and oil would be released down those pipes to create what might look like a giant version of a frying pan fire. Huge flames would whoosh up into the night sky. This replicated what a city target being hit by a bomb and exploding might look like. The idea was that any second or third wave of bombers would see these sudden dramatic flares and take this to be the target that earlier crews had aimed for.

*Very special effects: the ingenious Starfish Boiler that simulated
bomb hits.*

Another conjuring trick involved 'fire baskets' that had
square metallic bases with metal meshes through which
fires were detonated, and these were intended to mimic
the effect of flame and smoke pouring out of shattered
windows and doorways. Again this was all triggered by
careful electrical cabling. There were a great many of
these fire baskets, laid out in carefully calculated grids
based upon the topography of Bristol. They were interspersed with other electrical devices that simulated the
sparks from factory workshops, and even the rear red
lights of railway locomotives.

And there were dozens of these sites around the
country. It was a completely clandestine yet wholly visible

contribution to civil defence. It is difficult to estimate how many lives were saved by bombers being lured off course by these extravagant displays, or how many factories, power stations and homes escaped destruction. Nonetheless, even if the Luftwaffe became wise to the deceptions (as British aircrews were to similar German efforts), they were still a magnificent feat of resistance.

Very little survives in terms of infrastructure in these locations, but on top of Black Down, the operating bunker is still there, surrounded by those Neolithic burial chambers. The intense theatricality of this wartime secret – with night-time lighting effects that were seen by locals from miles around – somehow gains an extra resonance on understanding the archaeology of the site: the old warriors in their atavistic resting places right next to and beneath where the warriors of their future fought to defend their land. Certainly the area is a powerful draw for many local walkers now.

And of the many wartime secret landscapes, this is also one of the more heart-warming because the mad ingenuity and execution of the idea had more than a touch of Ealing Comedy about it: the boffin technicians in their blast-proof bunker, full of resolve despite the deep drone of enemy bombers overhead and taking energetic delight in igniting that vast set of illusory fires. Ultimately, they were inviting Luftwaffe planes to drop bombs directly on them, and so here was a secret that combined proper courage with an impossibly ancient delight in starting vast fires.

How to get there

The nearest small town, Charterhouse, is on the B3134 and the walking route to Black Down is signposted at the crossroads. For cycling enthusiasts, the area is just two miles from the Sustrans National Cycle Route 3.

A Night on the Moonlit Moors

Forest Moor and Menwith Hill, Yorkshire

Not all of wild Yorkshire is wuthering; some moors are relatively genteel. A few miles outside the wonderfully smart
town of Harrogate – the world's capital city of afternoon
tea – the land rises up into a prospect of broom and gorse
and thick clumps of woodland. Indeed, close to one such
patch of forest is a high wire fence, denoting a restricted
establishment. It has been this way for quite a long time.
But it was during the war that this site reached its peak of
hustle and bustle and to-ing and fro-ing. It was an inland
Naval base: HMS Forest Moor. And it was here that young
women from right the way across the country would sit
throughout the night working with incredible speed to
track and record the German's encrypted messages.

This was one of the clandestine out-stations of the
Y Service, which produced material for the codebreakers
at Bletchley Park, drawn from every single theatre of war.
The Women's Royal Navy and ATS (Auxiliary Territorial
Service) volunteers recruited for Forest Moor, and other
stations that we will hear of elsewhere, were carefully
enlisted for nimbleness of wits and a certain psychic

hardiness – for their role, carried out across twenty-four-hour periods in three shifts, seven days a week, was onerous. This was a role that demanded not only rare skill, but also preternatural focus and concentration, and before they arrived at Forest Moor, they had already been through a full six months of the most intensive training at a special centre on the Isle of Man.

As each Forest Moor shift began, the women had to take up positions by radio receivers, put on their headsets, ready their log pads (with carbon paper, to create instant copies) and tune into the German radio operators who were firing out messages at incredible speeds. The minds of the Y Service women were – for these seven-hour shifts – filled entirely with the dots and dashes of Morse code. They instantly translated these pulses of sound into letters, and they wrote down these letters in groups of five on their specially lined pads. The messages they spelled out were encrypted and this was the raw material that would be sent on at top speed to Bletchley. There was no let-up, and no room for error. This was not an abstract exercise. Each of these young women, sitting in huts high up on those moors on moonlit nights, knew that the work they were doing could mean the difference between life and death.

The recruits to this secret world had sometimes been approached in the course of their ordinary Wren naval training (which itself could range widely from simple marching exercises to complex courses in subjects such as radio operation and meteorology). Some disclosed in their interviews that they liked nothing better than to unwind with fiendish cryptic crosswords. There were just as many who not only had an aptitude for complex mathematics but actually a love for the discipline. Others let it be known that they were super-keen on working with hi-tech equipment. Pat Sinclair, who as a north London teenager watched the Blitz of the city from the suburban hills above, was driven to join the Y Service not merely out of patriotic duty but also out of a passion for electrics. The science of radio fascinated her, and luckily, she was to learn a staggering amount about 'ohm's and about how radio waves flowed and bounced off the stratosphere. This she had in common with many other volunteers. It wasn't just a matter of taking down dictation in Morse code; this was acquiring the skill and sensitivity to identify individual German radio operators, and to hunt down the signals they sent based on their unique operational style, wherever in the world they had been sent from.

Such work today would be associated with computer whizzes, working in a blur of speed to pull off seemingly impossible coups of communication. These women were working directly to help shorten the war. Not that they could know precisely how; the nature of Bletchley Park was kept just as secret from them as it was from everyone else. Sometimes the initials 'BP' would be heard and there would be flurries of speculation about what they could stand for. Were all their captured messages being sent on to Buckingham Palace? Baden Powell? Only many years after the war were they to learn the truth.

And they were doing their bit to save the nation in circumstances that were not glamorous. The Forest Moor base, far from even the most inquisitive locals, was spartan at the best of times. One woman recalled, with a shudder, how when she arrived in its earliest days, the outdoor lavatories were primitive in the extreme. There were not even doors – simply hanging scraps of khaki cloth. In the sleet and the hail, the route between huts on slippery duckboards was a maze of wetness. In the middle of the night, in the blackout (naturally, here, like everywhere else in the country, they were under the very strictest instructions not to show even a glimmer of light), calls of nature could become howling elemental challenges.

Food, also, could sometimes be a little ad hoc. One secret listener recalled the end of a gruelling shift being marked with the offer of a cold, congealed baked-bean sandwich. Perhaps mercifully, the women who were sent to Forest Moor did not live on site; instead, they were a few miles away in a requisitioned girls' boarding school called St Ethelburga's. But their world was still rather circumscribed. A shift on Forest Moor began with the transport truck arriving and the drive up there in the winter was not always perfectly straightforward. Thick fogs could sometimes enwreathe the roads and the slow-moving trucks could topple, with little dignity, into roadside ditches.

But in the summer, even this most uninspiring prospect of Nissen huts, arrays of aerials and a vast static water tank in the middle (simply there in case any fire broke out) could soften a little. It was acknowledged that sunshine was important for secret listeners, who otherwise spent most of their time crouched indoors behind black-out windows. There were grassy spaces where listeners could go before or after shifts to lie back in the heather-scented warm. Equally, the countryside around the base was perfect walking and picnic territory: a riot of rare plants and earthy bog and sun-warmed boulders, the air filled with the songs of redstarts, flycatchers, cuckoos, curlews and meadow pipits.

Added to this, Harrogate had a rather superior cultural life, certainly compared with many other towns around the country. Some secret listeners recalled the much sought-after pleasures of good concerts, repertory theatre and indeed amateur dramatics, which were like escapist balm after the iron grip of their relentless routine.

Meanwhile, the senior commanders had to find some ingenious means of maintaining morale on site at Forest Moor, to help prevent burn-out. Wren Anne Stuttford remembered a ruse that was almost moving in its simplicity. 'Our lieutenant, Hancock was his name, fashioned a medal,' she said. 'It was a hideous thing made of cardboard with red squiggles on it and a red ribbon. As one of us found a "missing group" [prized enemy radio frequencies which had been changed and lost], so the medal was stuck on her [radio] set. So fierce was the competition for this medal, it could have been made of solid gold . . . I wonder if Hancock realised what a clever ploy that was, so many spirits kept up by a small circle of cardboard.'

On the warm May night before the war came to an end, there were Wrens and ATS girls who remembered being driven in those old army trucks up to Forest Moor, reporting for duty and settling themselves down before the familiar Bakelite dials, the heavy earphones in position. But they were surprised by there being very little for them to listen to – just random messages issuing from Germany, and nothing coherent. They remembered that there was a definite turn in the atmosphere, a sense that the world was different. The women coming in to relieve them for the midnight shift were laughing and in giddy spirits and told their colleagues to put on dark glasses. Why? As the evening-shift listeners walked out of the radio room, they were greeted with the extraordinary sight of the midnight base bathed all around in light. The blackout was at an end.

And the next day, in the warmth of that spring and amid all the trees and the moors, they recalled that when the official news of Victory in Europe arrived, very suddenly, the Forest Moor base that was previously so austere and stark, suddenly took on an entirely new and friendly feel. Numbers of women gathered around the huge static water tank. Some sang 'There'll Always Be an England', while numbers of Scottish recruits countered with 'As long as Scotland's there'.

Curiously, this corner of the world never stopped being secretive. Indeed, in the years after the war, the layers of secrecy unusually multiplied. Close to Forest Moor is a site which has the honour of being perhaps

Spheres of influence: RAF Menwith Hill.

one of the most closely guarded clandestine sites in the country today. RAF Menwith Hill is a science-fictional prospect of giant white golf balls, dominating the horizon of the moor, stretching off into the distance. These are radomes. And this site has multiple high-security functions, not least of which is missile warning. Today communications interception of course extends far into cyberspace, and outer space too, via satellites. And the base, while falling under the aegis of the Ministry of Defence, is one of the more concrete symbols of the special relationship between Britain and America with the base being largely staffed with American intelligence operatives.

Bearing all that in mind, it is perhaps understandable that this establishment has never welcomed weekend walkers, or indeed anyone wearing cagoules. But from a distance, while out on the wind-buffeted moors and contemplating the rich history of espionage here, it is difficult to imagine anyone in that futuristic-looking sci-fi city having to use lavatorial facilities cloaked only with a khaki cloth, or indeed to find that supper is a cold-baked-bean sandwich.

How to get there

There are lots of subtle pleasures in the rural landscape to be found around Forest Moor and Menwith Hill, although one might have to keep an eye out for boggle-eyed conspiracy theorists convinced that the Menwith Hill establishment has made contact with aliens. The nearest railway station is Harrogate (itself always worth visiting), which has frequent connections to York. RAF Menwith Hill lies just off the A59. Turn north up Hardgroves Hill for Forest Moor.

SECRET COASTLINES

They Do Like to Spy
Upon the Seaside

Irton Hill, Scarborough, Yorkshire

A town that in days of peace attracted thousands of holidaymakers a year was, in war, almost wholly transformed.
The grand resort of Scarborough, on the Yorkshire coast,
might have seemed to some to be rather out of the way.
But it was filled with troops and Wrens, there for a whole
raft of different operational reasons. It received some serious bombing raids, with terrible casualties and damage,
and the local fishing trawlers were regularly attacked by
German craft. Yet somehow, amid all the mayhem of
conflict, the town's old sunny nature kept on stubbornly
reasserting itself. For those who worked at a top-secret
establishment a little up the hill from the town, the
opportunities for dancing and horse-riding were greatly
appreciated. This was the cohort of young women who
would prove instrumental in searching the oceans and
tracking down the famous German battleship *Bismarck*,
leading to one of the war's most memorable coups. It was
some compensation for the arduous underground life that
they were required to lead.

Though Scarborough was related to many other secret listening stations around the country, the one here had particular significance. There had been such a station at the town since 1912, eavesdropping on all manner of shipping out at sea, and monitoring the movements of any vessels that could prove hostile. The station was originally based in Sandybed Lane. As the Second World War came, it was to see the most startling influx of fresh and intelligent new recruits. And it was also going to have to burrow beneath the earth, because German bombers had been swift to see that Scarborough as a town had a great deal of military activity and significance.

Come 1943, the new base on Irton Moor, overlooking the steel-grey North Sea, was a crucial link in the world-wide chain of coded messages that led all the way back to Bletchley Park. What distinguished this site was – as some recalled – both its claustrophobia and its intense smokiness. That was an age in which most adults smoked cigarettes, in every location and at every opportunity. Even the most air-conditioned bunkers were bound to get a little hazy.

That was not the worst of it, as Wren Norah Phyllis Morgan recalled. The atmosphere of the base was strained. She herself had been pulled into 'special duties' due to her aptitude for speedy shorthand, an indicator of deftness with Morse code. Indeed, her own Morse speed was an impressive thirty words a minute (a more ordinary rate was twelve to fifteen words per minute). She was drafted to various stations in the north-east, gaining

The evocative remains of coastal defences near Scarborough.

experience with teleprinters, before being lined up for the hyper-confidential work at Scarborough.

One difficulty, she remembered, was that there were more people working there than had originally been intended, so the conditions were rather crowded. Alongside the perpetual fug of tobacco in the air, it was also uncomfortably warm as there was a great deal of electrical equipment, all of it giving off pulsing heat. The hours were an ordeal as well: sometimes the Wrens had to report for morning shifts, leave at 1 p.m., rest for the afternoon and then report back again for a nine-hour night shift stretching from 11 p.m. right the way through to 8 a.m. Perhaps if the work had been more varied, there might have been some relief, but the machine-like transcription of encoded Morse was relentless.

Unusually, there was also a commander in Ms Phyllis Morgan's time who seemed very hostile towards the idea of women working in his base. Given the amazing work that women across the country were doing in all sorts of roles, he seemed something of a dinosaur. Upon reporting for work, young women would be peremptorily pointed towards receivers and if anyone was off sick (there was a lot of stress-related illness on this and other sites), then someone like Ms Phyllis Morgan would be expected to position herself between two receivers, with an earphone from each in each of her ears.

But despite all these difficulties, there was also a chance for many to feel a great deal of pride at having been recruited to this base. It played a crucial role in intercepting messages sent from U-boats and other German vessels. As such, it was instrumental in protecting the convoys and keeping the nation's supply lines firm. As mentioned, it was at Scarborough that the whereabouts of the *Bismarck* was established after it had evaded British pursuers. As one of the largest and most prestigious battleships that had ever been built, this Nazi flagship was a fearsome threat in the naval war, and its destruction was vital to both the convoys and to morale. The Royal Navy renewed the chase through the waters of the Atlantic as the *Bismarck* set its course for St Nazaire, and eventually after terrifying torpedo exchanges, the mighty battleship was vanquished and sunk. But at Scarborough, even the more day-to-day work was invaluable. Wrens recalled how the encryptions they transcribed were picked up by naval officers and then bundled into packages and sent shooting off in vacuum tubes.

And after the intense effort, with the relentless hours and the need for mental engagement at all times, the bomb-battered Scarborough still held out all sorts of pleasurable escapist outlets for these secret heroines. The Olympic Ballroom – that earlier in the war had stipulated that dancers had to wear their gas-masks at all times, which must have resulted in the least romantic dances imaginable – was fully open and welcoming Wrens and great quantities of soldiers who were also billeted in the town.

The plush hotels had all been requisitioned. Some of the secret listening Wrens found themselves living in the Hotel Cecil, with others overlooking the seafront in the Grand. Naturally there was no room service and many Wrens shared each room. But some recalled how, thanks to their youth, this was their first real experience living away from home. And the communal nature of life here, although taking some adjusting to, eventually became a terrific source of spiritual support when work up at the secret listening HQ became a bit much. The beach itself was, for the duration of the war, largely off-limits aside from early mornings and afternoons (this was because of armed patrols and other fortifications against possible enemy landings) but it was still possible to hire horses to take off into the surrounding countryside.

While the soldiers and their training routines were self-explanatory, no one could fathom what all these young women in their naval uniforms were doing living in these hotels and then, before the start of each shift, assembling in queues to get on specially commissioned double-decker buses. These buses would take them up to the Y Service base. The unheeding locals imagined, with some rage, that these young ladies were being taken on grand outings for picnics rather than being put through their gruelling work to help the war effort.

Even though the listening base was in a bunker, there were still occasional hazards to face. One Wren recalled how after some German bombers had flown over in the depths of a winter night, she found herself up top having to swipe away incendiaries with a broomstick. Back below, an officer unaware of this angrily asked her why she had deserted her post. She told him in politely forthright terms.

For all the stress (everyone knew that a message missed could prove lethal and yet 'we couldn't ask the German operators to repeat the message'⁵, as one Wren put it), the pay was quite handsome. And even though they had no idea at the time, when it became apparent many years later that they had been part of the great clandestine code-breaking triumph, many former Wrens were allowed that wonderful belated glow of pride.

The Scarborough base had moved to larger premises in 1943, beneath the site of what had been the old racecourse. Even as the war came to an end, and the Wrens drifted back to their former lives, many operatives remained.

The listening station was still in a crucial position and in an uncertain new world, the movements of shipping and aircraft still had to be very closely monitored. The base – with its motley collection of Nissen huts and rather drab underground control room – was sufficiently far removed from the town as to not be a subject of general conversation. Indeed, the town itself was rather far removed, apart from in the summer months.

And there is still a base there today, not shrouded in the deep secrecy of the past but still relatively circumspect. It is now GCHQ Scarborough, and many in the town are intensely proud that this totem of history stands on Irton Moor. Not too long ago, it celebrated its centenary. As time goes by, more details of the base's Cold War years will be released. But that period of the war when thousands of young women threw themselves into the arduous complexities of Direction Finding also remains a great source of pride.

HOW TO GET THERE

Irton Moor lies just a few miles to the south of Scarborough. The nearest railway station is Seamer, itself a couple of miles away. The GCHQ base there is perfectly – and appropriately – undistinguished, and as with Menwith, might well be a magnet for a certain genre of obsessives. But the town of Scarborough itself, which all those Wrens enjoyed so much, is well worth visiting (the railway line has connections to York). It has retained much of its old charm.

The Sands of Destiny

Braunton Burrows, North Devon

The winds that whoosh along this expanse of the north Devon coast can catch the breath and make the heart jump. Yet the green undulating inland landscape – with its hills and deep hollows, crystal rivers and rich red soil – seems to suggest deep comfort. For the hundreds of American GIs billeted to the area around Barnstaple and Great Torrington from 1943, here was a remote but intensely welcoming corner of England typified by inns with log fires, lethally strong scrumpy and energetic dances in local halls. Though their purpose here was broadly secret, that they were training was plainly obvious to all locals. But they were not to know what these young men were specifically training for.

The Allied invasion of Europe was an extraordinary fusion of logistical ingenuity and vast individual, personal courage. The projected Normandy landings had to be rehearsed in the most intense detail. Allied troops would have to undergo the most comprehensive training with every conceivable beach-head scenario hurled at them. Men would have to learn the most effective means of attacking and defending from the second they jumped from those rocking craft and hit the wide, open sands. For all the technological advances of the conflict, in the hours before battle, every heart was the weight of iron, a feeling as old as war itself. Training will have drawn the mind to that crossing of the shadow line, the moment of the assault starting, amid molten gunfire and explosions, and the survival instincts required to work with a combination of intelligence and strength amid the chaos. For this mighty purpose, many beaches in the south of England were already being used by British soldiers – and tens of thousands of Americans were assigned to a vast area of pale sand dunes in north Devon. As it would transpire, this silent landscape was an almost perfect stand-in for Omaha Beach in Normandy.

Many of the troops to be put through the most vigorous training – from landing crafts to taking out enemy snipers in pill-boxes – were billeted in the nearby village of Braunton. Braunton Burrows, as the area of dunes was called, became the 'Assault Training Centre'. The land was owned by the Christie estate and was gladly given up to the military. It was here, amid other south Devon beaches, that the future course of the war was decided.

One of the challenges was acclimatising the men to the turbulent practicalities of disembarking from landing crafts in surging waters, and wading directly into bloody battle. With concrete mock-ups of landing craft constructed in the sands of the Burrows the men underwent exercises to ensure they had the effective means to leave them at speed, while facing hostile fire. Even this unrealistic and stable construction must have set adrenaline flowing, at the easily imagined reality to come.

High on the dune peaks in the hummocky grasses and hollows, there were specially constructed pill-boxes from which the Nazi defences were simulated. And there was more – in fact the noise and pyrotechnics will likely have driven the local schoolchildren wild with avid curiosity – for elsewhere in that labyrinth of high dunes, there were bazooka target grounds, flamethrower training areas and explosives used for demolishing obstacles and barbed wire. There were also special blast walls, soon pitted with the scars of live ammunition. Nothing could be left to chance; the Burrows also replicated the landscape that would render each soldier nakedly vulnerable and it was essential they were taught a variety of lethal means to subdue those who sought to kill them.

Near to this area of coastline, secret experiments were being carried out with some admirably inventive technology. There was PLUTO, a fantastic idea to keep the Allied forces securely supplied with fuel as the invasion of Europe began. It was an acronym: Pipe Lines Under The Ocean. In Watermouth Harbour, locals will have had a view of an enormous drum, the size of a house, floating in the waters. This was the means by which miles of cable would be laid out upon the floor of the Channel. Tests were carried out between north Devon and south Wales. Essentially these were the same sorts of cables that had previously been used to carry telecommunications wires.

The start of a special relationship: US troops in Britain were instructed in pub etiquette.

But these were hollow and would instead be carrying fuel, safely concealed from the attentions of enemy shipping and submarines.

In amid the secrecy around the purpose of this extraordinary object, there were also ferocious official warnings when tests were being carried out: no one within a very wide radius was permitted to smoke under any circumstances. The experiments were a success, and as the D-Day invasion began, so too did PLUTO. In the months after the landings, as the Allies pushed through the freezing forests of Europe, it was estimated to have supplied almost ten per cent of the fuel for the invasion.

For so many of these troops who were still yet to face the enemy, the wild coastline – combined with their increasing familiarity with weapons that could send out great jets of flame or fire rockets – must have been sobering. Their experiences in the local pubs had the opposite effect. A famous American training film from the 1940s was made to guide these soldiers through the intricacies of British pub etiquette (avoid boastfulness, loudness and over-familiarity). What it did not do was warn against the power of cloudy scrumpy. Nonetheless, despite the sombre nature of their training duties, and the fact that they had crashed into an area that was generally quite rural and close-knit, the Americans came to be remembered with intense fondness. It was recalled by the civilians of north Devon – the local children, the evacuated children, the women and older people – that the American troops who came to stay among them for those few months were filled with infectious good humour and energy. They dispensed sweets among severely rationed schoolchildren and they swept young women on to extemporised dance floors in village halls.

No amount of rehearsal or preparation could ever match the searing reality these men were about to face. The benign dunes of Braunton Burrows could never wholly simulate a landscape in which death could come at lightning speed from any direction. Nor could concrete landing crafts built amid the sand ever bring on the profound nausea of those Channel crossings, or the profound fear as the land grew near. For a generation that has broadly never known physical conflict, it is often difficult to imagine how the courage was summoned in these circumstances. How it was possible to push on even as those around you were being pierced with bullets or dismembered by explosions. These were young men who were already thousands of miles from home and from their own loved ones and on the secret dunes of Braunton Burrows they were being taught to face the possibility of their own mortality. They learned these lessons with grace.

A great many of them never returned home. The sacrifices made by Allied soldiers – American, British, Indian, Canadian, Australian and so many others – now seem to belong to an impossibly distant age. Yet this corner of north Devon is happy to acknowledge its ghosts. Brigadier General Paul W. Thomson of the US Army was later to declare: 'If Waterloo was won on the playing fields of Eton, surely the sands of north Devon beaches contributed importantly to the success of the assault on the Normandy beaches.'[6]

There are fragments and memories to be seen now in the valleys of dunes. The concrete landing craft are still there, for instance, as indeed are the skeletal remains of the old target practice pill-boxes. It is heartening that the public body Historic England has ensured that the landing craft replicas have been listed, so that whatever happens, they will always be present in that sand as irremovable monuments to the incredible bravery that was summoned here. There is also the luxuriant range

Rehearsals for valour: concrete D-Day practice, landing craft at Braunton Burrows.

of wildlife that those Americans will have also seen: the bee orchids, the blue butterflies, the hundreds of red, orange and turquoise wildflowers that break out in extravagant summer efflorescences. Parts of this vast area are still used by the military; although it is not Ministry of Defence land, training is still carried out beyond the eyes of north Devon locals. So today's walkers have to be watchful for forthcoming notices of exercises. In other parts of the country, such restrictions might feel frustrating, but here, in the breath-snatching winds that fly along these headlands, they feel curiously, counter-intuitively reassuring.

HOW TO GET THERE

The town of Braunton lies on the A361 a few miles west of Barnstaple. There is a walking route to The Burrows signposted with the South West Coast Path. Barnstaple is the nearest railway station and trains from here wind through north Devon to connections at Exeter.

Island of Ghosts

Foulness Island, Havengore and Shoeburyness, Essex

There is something curiously haunting about the Thames Estuary and the marshlands against which those grey waters lap. It is not just the remoteness and the silence, broken occasionally by the questioning cries of wheeling birds and by the river slurping against rusting jetties. It is also a feeling of history – that this, as Joseph Conrad wrote in *Heart of Darkness*, was 'one of the dark places on the earth'. Two thousand years ago, ruthless Roman warriors sailed these waters, thirsty for conquest. Five hundred years ago, at Tilbury, Queen Elizabeth prepared her ships for war. This was the portal through which the treasures of the empire entered. And this was also the land where new weapons of war were tested.

Just a few miles to the east of Southend-on-Sea lies a bleak region which has, for over a century, echoed to the reports of gunshots and explosions. There is also an island, strictly restricted to this day, with shooting ranges and the remnants of a vast brutalist concrete castle. Yet this island also plays host to a small community of civilians, gathered in weather-boarded houses near a handsome nineteenth-century church. The wider area is called Shoeburyness and the island is named Foulness. During the war, this island faced out to a North Sea over which came flying Luftwaffe bombers, and later the streaking rockets of the V-2 weapons, their exhausts a bright and rich tangerine against the indigo night sky. What happened on Foulness Island was confidential, but the echoes can still be heard today.

In centuries past, this was land that was reclaimed from the sea: fertile, interspersed with waterways and looking out over the eerie stretches of the Maplin Sands that appeared silver under the grey skies, and from which the tides would retreat for vast distances. Other than boat, the only means of getting to Foulness Island was on foot by means of a natural causeway. But this path across the sands was also extremely dangerous as thick mists would render the whole world grey and the senses of direction would be lost. And as walkers began to move in circles in the eye-throbbing haze, tides would turn and the waters of the sea would begin to rush back in with a sort of greed, and at the most extraordinary speed. With the rising waters came swirling currents and any walker who had not made it back to land at this point would very likely be yanked away by the fierce waters, to drown. An additional hazard was the quicksand where they could find themselves sinking, followed by a cold salt suffocation. The path became known as the Broomway, because 'brooms' or sticks of wood were planted deep into the sands along its course to indicate to travellers that they were staying within safety. But in the thick sea fogs, even these markers were no guarantee. So even before the military arrived in this cut-off place, the area was known for its ghosts.

There are stories even now, from sailors as well as walkers. One author spent the night sleeping in a small cabin cruiser moored not far from this spot on the Thames Estuary. It might have been a quirk of the autumnal weather, of the rain and the wind, but that author found in her rocking berth that she could not sleep. There was a measureless sense of unease in that undulating dark and as the night went on, the author heard distinct human voices on the estuary wind, crying out. That unshakeable sense of unease can be found in Foulness Island and Havengore Creek. A feeling that is sharpened by the knowledge that even if you are permitted to walk here, you are not exactly welcomed, by nature nor by the authorities that still use the region.

For this was long established as an ideal place to test – in secret, far from the prying eyes of foreign spies – revolutionary weaponry. One Lieutenant Colonel Henry Shrapnel came to these lonely marshes in the late eighteenth century to experiment with a brand-new form of exploding cannonball that would detonate in mid-air. It is from him that the term 'shrapnel', denoting fragments from ordnance, derives. A smart military garrison was laid out at Shoeburyness in the nineteenth century including barracks and more elegant quarters for officers. Its role frequently was to test the weapons that were being developed closer to London at Woolwich Arsenal. By the time of the Crimean War in the mid nineteenth century, these sullen sands and hummocks of marshland were echoing to a variety of roars and percussive detonations.

And by the time of the Second World War, the work carried out at Shoeburyness and Foulness, always obscured from the wider public gaze, became yet more guarded. Lots of sensitive research was evacuated deeper into the countryside, especially as here the skies above were the entry point for the Luftwaffe. But the conflict also brought a great number of women into the area, with the Auxiliary Territorial Service. And it was 'the ATS Girls' who moved into the vanguard of working and testing a new generation of what were termed 'weird and wonderful' weapons, from innovative guns to bazookas, and larger ordnance yet. Here was the location for the testing of truly vast explosive devices. In addition to this, Foulness Island saw some monumental architectural works including a vast concrete fortress, intended as a gun emplacement, and down by the rippling sands were enormous concrete walls. These were intended as replicas of the concrete Atlantic Walls that had been built on the French coast and they were here so that they could be subjected to explosive experiments. How best to demolish them, and were new scientifically modulated explosives needed to do so?

In the years after the war, Shoeburyness, Foulness and Havengore became enveloped in ever greater shrouds of mystery as they were utilised as sites for Cold War testing and experimentation. The reason for the obscurity was atomic science; the most secret weapons of them all. The area was taken up as an Atomic Weapon Research Establishment. Naturally there were no mushroom clouds to be seen above the concrete huts, but the explosive machinery required to detonate Britain's post-war nuclear bombs was formulated amid these silent inlets. The terrifying weapons subsequently tested in the distant south seas throughout the 1950s came to be in part from the work done on this site.

The legacy of the secret war created unexpected repercussions for both Foulness and the wider community around Shoeburyness and Southend. There was a point in the early 1970s when the region around Maplin Sands was considered for a new international airport for London. It had already taken a great deal of time to extract unexploded Second World War weapons from beneath the water where occasionally there would be vast explosions as yet more Nazi ordnance was discovered. Eventually it was decided that the logistics of constructing a huge airport in such an unforgiving landscape would be altogether too daunting. And so, the military testing went on.

The area remains in use as a weapons experimentation ground. Services are now provided by QinetiQ – the double Q suggestive of a tribute to James Bond's gadget master. In a striking passage on their website about the area, they say that their weapons-testing work involves 'firing, shaking, rattling, rolling, dropping, heating and freezing equipment and munitions'.[7] They also state, with magnificent dryness, that when such testing is underway

The mysteries in the marshes: aerial detail of the weapons-testing establishment on Foulness Island.

local residents 'may notice'. But in fairness, they have been noticing for almost 200 years, and there are some wonderful archival photographs of absurdly vast cannons in the 1850s, the blasts of which must have been heard as far away as Westminster.

Foulness Island, accessible by bridge, is not open to the public except for certain rare days in the year. School visits are encouraged, for as well as all the wartime work, there is an archaeological history here that suggests that Foulness had a military past reaching back millennia. The Romans were thought to have an encampment here, as previously did the Britons that they had succeeded in subduing. Meanwhile, hardy walkers eager to at least see the Broomway (it is extremely unwise to tackle the haunted causeway without being in the company of an experienced guide - even in an era of GPS and potential rescuers pinpointing the phones of those in distress, those lethal tides and implacable white fogs can outpace any rescuing boat), may do so as long as they abide very strictly by the military rules outlined upon a hundred signs and underscored at innumerable barriers. One of the main stipulations: don't for heaven's sake pick anything up. You never know what might explode in your hand.

In post-war years, the Thames Estuary unfairly acquired a reputation for ugliness, derived from its heavy industry. The combination of this and a secretive military presence has meant that Shoeburyness, Foulness and Havengore have been something of an acquired taste for many visitors. But after many years, if not decades, of this estuarine landscape being viewed as bleak and forbidding and louring, eyes have been opened to its true beauty.

Shoeburyness, which was once simply the end of the line from London Fenchurch Street, has been re-purposed for residents and the old garrison buildings now have a scrubbed-up Victorian splendour with gateways, squares, handsome architecture and cobbles. Meanwhile the village of Churchend on Foulness Island still boasts traditional white weather-boarded housing and the lovely church forms part of an occasional visitor trail, usually on Sundays. Step out towards the lonely sands and you will now see an exuberance of madly thriving wildlife, from dancing avocets to grey seals watching all with measurelessly black eyes. Meanwhile, the scientists and the military men want the public to know that nothing disturbs the habitats of some of the area's prized bird species including the redshanks, the bar-tailed godwits, the oystercatchers and grey plovers.

These birds and animals have no interest in the old military secrets that echo all around them, and now that the industry and the noise that accompanied those secrets have largely disappeared, the wildlife has come to reassert itself.

How to get there

As is appropriate for such a secretive historic site, Foulness and Havengore, which lie just several miles to the north of Shoebury-ness, are an effort to get to. Foulness itself may only be visited on the first Sunday of the month from April to October, and even then, only between the hours of 12 p.m. and 4 p.m. Only the handful of residents are permitted to use the road bridge; general visitors must walk. And of course, here is where the starkest warnings must be issued. The path along to Foulness cannot be accessed from the Shoeburyness shore. You must make your way a couple of miles north to the village of Great Wakering. There, you can pick up the coastal path at Wakering Stairs pointing north, but ideally go with an experienced guide and certainly never ever try this alone or in bad weather. The Broom-way, as described, has its haunted reputation for a reason: fast inrushing tides and quicksand are ever present threats, as is the all-enveloping fog. The wet mud might also contain old, unexploded ordnance. But if you can make it through all of that – a very early start is also recommended, given the amount of time it will take to surmount all these obstacles – there are public footpaths that criss-cross Foulness which you are free to use.

Old Bones and Death Rays

Worth Matravers, near Swanage, Dorset

On a stretch of prehistoric coast, where the fossilised creatures embedded in the cliffs give a glimpse of an ancient world that was, the young pilots of the Luftwaffe occasionally swooped to strafe the living. Perhaps they calculated that they could have an impact, that their bullets might on the off-chance catch a scientist who was developing means of having their planes atomised as they flew. More likely was that this was the red fog of aggression stimulated by dog-fights in those crystal-blue skies. But on a remote tip of the Dorset headland, overlooking the wide Channel, there was indeed secret work being carried out that would be invaluable to fighters and bombers alike. Just outside a tiny village of limestone cottages called Worth Matravers was a research establishment that even by the early 1940s had had a peripatetic war.

This was the Telecommunications Research Establishment and it had moved at rather short notice. During the late 1930s, it had a home in Suffolk at the delightfully grand Bawdsey Manor. Here was where the great pioneering steps in radar – both defensive and offensive – were

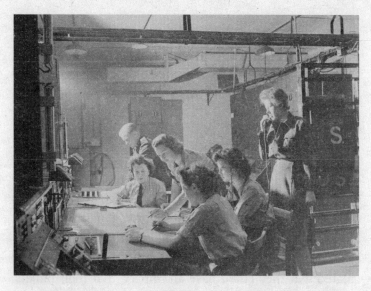

*High intensity: Flight Officer P. M. Wright supervises (right)
as Sergeant K. F. Sperrin and WAAF operators Joan Lancaster,
Elaine Miley, Gwen Arnold and Joyce Hollyoak work on the
plotting map in the Receiver Room at Bawdsey CH, Suffolk.*

taken, as the scientists watched aeroplanes test their new
machinery over the east coast seawaters. But these laboratories were within all too easy reach of any potential Nazi
attackers or invaders and so at the start of the war there
was a temporary move north of the border to Scotland.
This was improvisation, and occasioned simply because
the formidable radar pioneer Robert Watson-Watt happened to have gone to university there. However, there
was simply no room and the scientists had to move twenty
miles along the flowing River Tay to the charming town

of Perth, which had an airfield – RAF Scone – amid some pretty hills. But the infrastructure at this airfield was scanty and could not accommodate the sheer ambitious scale of the work that the boffins were doing. So, by the beginning of 1940 – just weeks before the Battle of Britain – it was time to move once more, and close to where some army colleagues were engaged in their own radar work.

The establishment was hurriedly assembled but looked striking – that is, for anyone who happened to be in what was essentially a rather cut-off vicinity. The nearest town was Swanage and a little to the north was Corfe Castle. But otherwise, this spur of the Dorset coast was almost timelessly set apart from the urban and industrial sprawl of England. Dominating the area were two vast masts, some 360 feet high. Around these twin needles of steel and wood were Nissen huts and one-storey workshops. The view from the chalky grassland out to the flint grey Channel was exhilarating. So too was the nature of the work.

Just a few years previously in the mid 1930s, some of the ideas that would conjoin fruitfully to point to a future of radar had in part originated with a rather simpler and more brutal suggestion: death rays. It was acknowledged that enemy bomber and fighter pilots were almost impossibly difficult to stop. Might there be the chance of inventing a lethal ray that could kill them stone dead at their controls?

While the answer to this was an emphatic no, scientists involved in radio research, most notably Watson-Watt, became intrigued by another possibility: that enemy planes might betray themselves by the energy that they gave off and that the 'echoes' of this energy might be detected via radio location, thus showing the defence forces their position and their course. It was from here that an entire new field of research – and defensive technology – blossomed. This was a new age of cathode rays and green blips on grey screens. And in this corner of Dorset, there were very few around to see the occasional flashes, like lightning, that came from this cluster of wooden huts whenever an electrical experiment ran slightly out of control.

As with most secret wartime establishments, there was an air of youthful energy. Young technicians worked very long hours – and frequently seven-day weeks – with WAAFs (the volunteers for the Women's Auxiliary Air Force). The boffins were more than usually proactive, the new radar equipment naturally had to be tested out in flight and from a nearby extemporised airfield, the scientists would often take off as passengers in Blenheims and Mosquitoes. They were sometimes more heedlessly daredevil than the experienced pilots, asking for instance that their planes be flown very low over the Channel waters – as low as fifty feet above the waves. Meanwhile, in terms of living arrangements, there was not enough room in the hamlet of Worth Matravers for even the modest numbers of people gathered there, though some did find lodgings at nearby farms. Instead, many of them were ferried back and forth to Swanage, which despite its own relative

Keep scanning the skies: the moving radar memorial at
St Aldhelm's Head near the former Worth Matravers HQ.

smallness, came to be relished by many for its dances and (limited) nightlife.

There was a young man – a self-styled boffin – called James Rennie Whitehead, who was one of the fearless experimental aviators at Worth Matravers. He had the fondest memories of this most active secret research base. There was one occasion he recalled when a German fighter pilot decided to launch an attack on the compound. There was one scientist, he wrote, who had been sitting in his wooden hut laboratory when a bullet came through the ceiling and pierced a metal cabinet. The scientist practically jumped through the roof with fright as that bullet ricocheted with the most astonishing racket in that cabinet before coming to rest.

Mr Whitehead also remembered the brilliance of the WAAF women who worked there, peering into those dull grey and green screens and – like fortune tellers gazing into crystal balls – divining the distance and timing of approaching enemy raids. Theirs was a realm of cathode ray tube displays and devices called goniometers. And these women formed part of a link that stretched around the coast – the Chain Home system (this was a ring of pioneering early-warning radar stations in strategic spots, notable for their vast pylons). Some worked in conditions less congenial and even more remote than Worth Matravers. But this site was special because of its secret scientific advances.

It might have been coincidence – for the Germans could not have known with any certainty about the work that was being done there – but the aerial attacks intensified as the months went on. The sedate resort of Swanage itself was machine-gunned from the air and there were fatal casualties. For this, among other reasons, the Telecommunications Research Establishment was set to move again by 1942, this time to the Worcestershire town of Great Malvern. But it was to leave behind a pleasing legacy of a time when senior Whitehall scientists and RAF high command would come down to this little seaside town for the weekend both to assess the progress made in fully functioning radar that would enable bombers to pinpoint targets hundreds of miles away with uncanny accuracy, and also to breathe in the sea airs of the beautiful, fossilised coast.

HOW TO GET THERE

Worth Matravers itself is still a ludicrously pretty village and its natural setting amid the nearby wild cliffs and the blue ocean – plus the old churches and close-by Corfe Castle – make it ideal for extended mooching. In terms of transport, it is a little out of the way, and so driving is pretty much the only option. It lies just over a mile to the west of Swanage, just off the B3069. The nearest railway station, Wareham, is on the Bournemouth line, and is roughly ten miles way.

The Poisoned Isle

Gruinard, Ross and Cromarty, Scotland

For all the glorious stories of the spirit of wartime, the shadows are never far behind. One of the darkest of those shadows was cast over a tiny little island off the north-west of Scotland. And for decades, it remained a poisoned reminder of the deathly reality of the conflict. Into a landscape of almost transcendent beauty was brought an obscenity of a weapon that no one ever wanted to use, and which all sides feared. Other secret coastlines and wildernesses in those war years had a redemptive touch of romanticism, a sense of life-loving humanity. Here was an island that came to symbolise the bleakest nihilism. Thoroughly secret during the war years, its terrible truth had to be disclosed shortly afterwards to the public, lest curious visitors fall victim to its lethal soil.

The island is called Gruinard and it is possible to visit it today without fear of falling victim to its toxic legacy. It is a mound of treeless green and pebbled grey, overlooked in the distance by mighty hills. It is about one mile in length, and half a mile wide, and is within rowing distance of the mainland. The closest town – as the crow flies, as opposed to the meandering mainland road – is Ullapool. In 1942, contemplating a hideous future escalation of weaponry into chemical warfare, and the seeming impossibility of protecting a vulnerable domestic population, it was decided to use this scrap of land as an experiment. Sit on the beach facing across to it now and no one could ever guess what had happened there.

A group of biologists and chemists who had been working at the ultra-secret research establishment at Porton Down in Wiltshire made the journey hundreds of miles north. Heading northwest from Inverness, the land gradually shoulders into dark mountains, vast fir-lined glens and stretches of icy loch. Gruinard was a short boat voyage from the sandy shores that overlook it and on those boats were both scientists and requisitioned sheep. What happened to those sheep was captured on film, which itself remained completely confidential until about twenty years ago. Even in the fragments we can see now, it does not make for easy viewing.

The animals were locked into wooden stocks, their heads held firm. Around them scientists in pale yellow protection suits, with vast helmets, set the devices. The detonations, via mortar, looked relatively modest, seen as puffs of ash-grey smoke. Following the detonations, the sheep were freed to roam the island. It took several days before the results became apparent. Those animals that had been closest to the puffs of smoke were dead. Those that remained alive did not have much longer to live. Most were then incinerated. Some were buried. There were, apparently, a few that had already made their way in deathly delirium to the sea, and were now being pulled, lifeless, back and forth by the strong local currents.

This was an experiment with anthrax, which is a form of bacteria that occurs quite naturally in very low levels in the skin and the fur of some animals. But even microscopic amounts in the air can be harmful with prolonged exposure and it had been noted in decades past that some shepherds and others who worked in the wool trade sometimes fell victim to what was known as 'Woolsorter's Disease'. It began as the anthrax made its way through their skin. The initial symptoms were similar to influenza: a sense of profound tiredness, coughing, a vice-like pressure on the chest and a rising fever. In addition to this though was the recognised token of the disease which was a growing boil on the skin at the point where the bacteria had made its entry. The boil would get to a point where it had a black centre, like a bullseye.

The terror was that the Nazis, in desperation at waning fortunes and the attrition of fighting on eastern as well as other fronts, would unleash anthrax bombing on civilians. Instead of pouring fiery incendiaries on cities like London, Birmingham, Liverpool and Southampton, the planes instead would be armed with anthrax bombs, which would explode and send lethal spores over millions of people. In such a case, the illimitable deaths would be painful and horribly prolonged. After inhalation, there could be blood poisoning or internal bleeding, as well as hideously drawn-out breathing difficulties. This was a threat against which there was no vaccine, no inoculation.

Equally, though, British scientists were being commissioned to fashion this deadly weapon first. One idea floating around was that Germany might be targeted with the bacteria in such a way that not only could humans fall victim, but vast swathes of cattle too. It was thought that it might be possible to kill off Germany's livestock, thus bringing its people to the edge of famine. It was reasoned that the end of the war would follow swiftly after.

The island of Gruinard was owned by Mollie and Peter Dunphie. Although it had had no human inhabitants since the nineteenth century, it had been noted as a popular day-tripping spot for highland tourists. Local fishermen also liked to rest there under the warm summer sun. All of this was to end. The island was requisitioned by the War Office and the Dunphies received £500 for their trouble.

And in 1942, this lonely island and its wildlife were poisoned so that the authorities could try to face their fears of chemical attacks. To see if there was some way, having spread these spores, that they could divine a means to counter their deadly effects. It was a means of staring into the darkest abyss but there was no scientific comfort to be drawn here. The sheep died and the spores remained, horribly resilient, even in this storm-exposed corner of the world. The very few people who lived in the nearby mainland at first had no inkling of what had been done on Gruinard, but soon there were unsettling local stories of dead animals washing up on beaches close by.

*Two men, both wearing protective clothes, stand by a sign
on Gruinard Island during a visit to the highly restricted
government-acquired Scottish island, circa 1950.*

One dead sheep was set upon by an eager dog and before
long, that dog too was dead. Gruinard was now an island
of death and having unleashed this weapon, there was no
way that the scientists could kill it.

Despite locals seeing these signs, as the war progressed,
what had happened there had to be kept a close secret.
So even as metal signs were erected around Gruinard
forbidding anyone to set foot on it because of the hazard
of poisoning, a wider official silence fell. And that silence
was filled with fearful local speculation. The owner of the

dog that had died reported the upsetting mystery and the authorities instantly saw to it that he received handsome financial compensation.

And after the war, as the warning signs remained, the island became a source of wider urban rumours. There were holidaymakers familiar with the area disappointed that they were no longer allowed to row out to their favourite isolated picnic area. But the authorities were implacable. It was believed that once anthrax was in the soil, it could contaminate it for many generations to come. If anyone were to set foot on the island, they would not only be in the gravest individual danger but they could get spores attached to their footwear or clothes which they then might unwittingly take back to the mainland. Every year, a group of scientists in hazmat suits went back to Gruinard to take samples of the earth. Every year they found that it was still deadly. And any continental tourists who sailed too close were warned off by official vessels.

Despite the intense confidentiality, rumours began to solidify into objective fact. By the late 1970s and early 1980s, the island was receiving chilling attention from those who sought to use the toxic soil for their own ends. A specialised terror cell posted soil from Gruinard to the Conservative Party HQ and the research establishment at Porton Down. The aim of this cell was apparently to make the government clean up the island. The perpetrators were never caught.

In hindsight, there was something faintly absurd as well as sinister about having such a lethal area so very close to the mainland. A few years after that, it seemed that there might just be the technological means to make the island safe again. Over the years, every time a boat got into trouble in the area, the newspapers always referred starkly to 'the Forbidden Isle'. It was a horrible secret in plain sight. By the late 1980s, a team was sent to Gruinard to sluice it with industrial chemicals and seawater. It took time for the efficacy of the treatment to become apparent. When it did, a ceremony was decided upon. In 1990, Whitehall sent a junior minister up to north-west Scotland to clamber on board a small boat to make the short crossing, set foot on the cleansed island and to declare it free of the poison.

Gruinard became popularly known as Anthrax Island. Today it has not entirely shaken off its sinister reputation. Even now there are those who would be a little reluctant to actually set foot on it. For daredevils, however, there are some adventurous options, including organised kayaking trips around the waters of the island, with a chance to moor on one of its beaches and explore it. This is a corner of Secret Britain with perhaps the darkest history, but what seems even more remarkable now is the way that the memories of such terrible experiments can eventually be washed away.

How to get there

This is a serious proposition, befitting a long summer holiday and possibly also a campervan. To reach the mainland point of Gruinard Bay, the wiggly road to take around the coastline is the A832. The area has a variety of accommodation. The nearest railway station is a considerable distance away: Garve, on the Inverness branch line to the Kyle of Lochalsh. There are canoeing firms near the island that organise guided paddling.

The Storm Hunters in the Shingle

Orford Ness, near Aldeburgh, Suffolk

In centuries to come, it is possible that future archaeologists, crunching over these pebbles under an illimitable grey sky, will be intensely puzzled by the fragments of structure that remain in this lonely landscape. It's true that the pagoda-shaped concrete pavilions, the curved outbuilding roofs half-submerged under accumulated slopes of shingle and the wide steel circles embedded in the ground are a slightly odd sight. The people of Suffolk who lived in houses overlooking this spit of land lying between the rushing River Alde and the wide sea beyond, were likely even more puzzled when the buildings were in use. This stony spur is close to the town of Orford and not far from the artistic centre of Aldeburgh. As Benjamin Britten composed close by, there were teams of boffins bustling around laboratories in the middle of the night, conducting experiments and research that were to help change the course of the war. Orford Ness continued to present a secretive face to the world long after the conflict. Now it is revered by walkers and tourists attracted to the more obscure corners of British history.

Rather like Foulness Island, the possibilities of Orford Ness had been apparent to military minds for a very long time. Both alluringly remote and sufficiently close to railways offering fast journeys to London, here was an ideal location for physicists to work in both freedom and silence, far from interference and indeed far from inquisitive eyes. Just before the outbreak of the First World War, Whitehall acquired the land – in previous centuries a favourite with smugglers – with the idea of using it for aviation research. The offensive and defensive capabilities of the earliest aircraft were still being fathomed during this time, and they decided here was the space for their airfields and laboratories.

It also became a workshop of dazzling creation. Out on this cut-off limb of land, scientific inspiration seemed wholly uninhibited. After the First World War, the land was retained for an amazing array of experiments. How best was night-flying to be achieved? Why, by finding a way of illuminating the instruments. How best could aeroplane crews fight the deadly cold of night flights? How about flight suits that could be electrically heated? It was at Orford Ness that the delicate workings of parachutes were perfected, so that pilots could survive falling thousands of feet, and it was here too that plane crews were instructed in the new espionage art of aerial photography. Some soon-to-be distinguished scientific names took that ferry across the River Alde and crunched their way along the shingle. Among them were Henry Tizard and Frederick Lindemann. Both would play key roles in the Second World War.

And indeed, it was in the years leading up to 1939 that Orford Ness acquired deeper and more lasting significance. The work carried out in these laboratories of brick facing out over the night sea produced astounding advances in science. For some years, the spit had been used for the testing of ballistics, and bombs were routinely dropped out at sea. But in the mid 1930s, prompted by the leaping advances made by Henry Tizard, rector of Imperial College, and his Aeronautical Research Committee, a scientist called Robert Watson-Watt, who we have met previously in Dorset, arrived with his team. No one was permitted to know their exact purpose. They were there apparently to start work on an 'Ionospheric Research Station' (the term suggesting the exploration of conditions in different layers of the atmosphere), repurposing some of the existing brick buildings. What they were in fact doing was putting together a new sort of defence system. The bomber would always get through, declared the Prime Minister Stanley Baldwin. But that did not mean that it would get through undetected. If the enemy could be pinpointed electronically, then fighters could be scrambled to meet him head on.

And so it was that radar was brought into pulsating life (and several years later was developed further and just as ingeniously by the Telecommunications Research Department, as we have seen) amid the crunching shingle and withering eastern winds of the spit. Very swiftly thereafter the work would be moved a little further up the coast to Bawdsey Manor – for some, a rather more congenial

Far-sighted: Sir Robert Alexander Watson-Watt (1892–1973) with the apparatus he developed to detect reflected radio echoes from enemy aircraft.

and marginally less vulnerable spot. But there were other secrets yet to be developed on the eerie Ness.

Inside these brick huts, the scientists watched darkening autumn skies and, like Frankenstein, they sought to harness the thunder storms that raged in across the North Sea. The aim here was the rather more innocent quest to eliminate radio interference for the RAF when such conditions hit. There was also work carried out on developing accurate technology for bomb sights (instruments which helped guide bomber planes towards their targets), a taste of the increasingly active role of Bomber Command and its limitlessly brave crews as they flew further into the darkness of Nazi Germany, seeking to end the war by bringing fire to German cities. At Orford Ness, there was also research into armour plating, where scientists worked on devising ever more ferocious ways of piercing durable casings.

Of course, there were Germans flying overhead here, and often Orford Ness and the nearby town of Orford happened to be on the return flight path for the Luftwaffe after they had bombed large city targets. The coastline below was their chance to offload any last bombs that remained. The town itself was hit, with fatalities. But there were also German planes brought down in the sea close by, their crews captured and taken prisoner.

Throughout the war, as Orford Ness also saw experimental trials to do with Barnes Wallis's Tallboy bombs (vast efforts designed to shatter the most fortified structures), plus testing of the assembly of Mulberry harbours (those astoundingly ingenious temporary artifical harbours that allowed troop ships to be unloaded), the local children – and those who had been evacuated from the London districts of Dagenham and Barking – were presumably frantic with curiosity. The spit could not be practically reached without a boat and the only other way around the river was to travel to Aldeburgh, and then turn back south to face the prospect of miles of uneven shingle. In the summer, the land and its buildings shimmered in the light and were easily seen, but in the autumn, they would frequently be invisible due to the silver sea mists. By the end of the war, they attained a metaphorical invisibility.

As top secret as it had been over the past few years, the advent of the Cold War brought it an extra – and some might think sinister – dimension.

In August 1945, a world that had already seen so much horror was faced with the detonation of America's atomic bombs over Hiroshima and Nagasaki. Politicians and generals now saw that entire cities could be destroyed with the speed of a flash of lightning. It was Clement Attlee's Labour government that was most insistent that Britain should have its own nuclear weapon as a deterrent and it was at Orford Ness in the years that followed that testing on detonation triggers was carried out. This was the era of the Atomic Weapons Research Establishment. Of course, there were no actual nuclear bombs on the spit itself, just the vital components, but the site was heavily guarded and the work within enveloped within deeper layers of confidentiality. Indeed, much of the secrecy remains to this day.

But locals and walkers in Suffolk could see, in that faraway haze towards the sea, the curious shapes of the new buildings that were starting to rise from the shingle. Those who worked at the Establishment often frequented the town of Orford but there was never any indication of the true significance of their work. In the 1960s, there was a partnership with the Americans that led to even more buildings on the spit. There was research carried out on the firing systems for missile projects such as Blue Danube and Blue Streak. The Americans meanwhile pursued Cobra Mist, a new and advanced form of radar technology. The local rumours, though, were pleasingly outlandish. Not convinced that anything so quotidian could be happening in such an unearthly spot, there was eventually a story that Orford Ness was concealing a secret that would change the very nature of all of life on earth and that within one of those strange buildings was a captured UFO.

Eventually, a few years ago, the research was wound down and Orford Ness was allowed to sink into an even deeper silence than before. Around the abandoned, empty laboratories and curved-roofed silos, huge piles of shingle were arranged, making some of the buildings resemble ancient ruins that had been partially dug out from beneath the stones. Rather than concealment this was done by means of defence: the sea on the eastern coast is aggressively advancing, and this was a simple way of preventing the collapse of vast concrete structures. A few years back, Orford Ness was taken over by the National Trust and as a much sought-after Holy Grail for walkers, the area was opened – to a certain extent. There were, however, good reasons to limit complete access to certain areas and unexploded ordnance was one of them. In addition, while the abandoned architecture may have a certain brutalist attraction – there is something weirdly tantalising about the very idea of abandoned secret concrete laboratories – it's deemed safer for the general public not to get too close. Several years back, there were members of some urban walking groups who were keen not only to explore these resonant relics of war, but also to spend the night among them.

The ghost citadel by the shore: The former Atomic Weapons
Research Establishment (AWRE) at Orford Ness in Suffolk.
It was used to test ordnance from the First World War
through to the Cold War.

Probably better that they never did; it could well have
been horribly unsettling. For as well as the ghostly nature
of these weird empty structures in this weird empty
place, there is also the inevitable recollection of one of
the world's most famous ghost stories, set on a long line
of shingle not very far from these abandoned labs. In
M. R. James's 'Oh, Whistle, And I'll Come To You, My
Lad' a walker passes along the nearby Felixstowe shingle
strand in deep twilight, all alone, and notices that there is
a figure in the distance, making its way along the pebbles
with hands slightly outstretched, as though blind, but also

moving in his direction with unnerving speed. The walker can't help but associate this uncanny approaching figure with an antique whistle that he had found and blown. The whistle bore a Latin inscription which translated thus: who is this who is coming? In another story, set in Aldeburgh and again unfolding on the beach near Orford Ness, a gentleman archaeologist who discovers an ancient Saxon crown – and who claims it for himself – is hunted down by a supernatural presence and, as a profound fog descends, meets a startlingly violent end.

The Orford Ness scientists who sat in those huts attempting to manipulate radio waves against mighty thunderstorms must themselves have felt that odd twinge of the *unheimlich*. Which is of course one of the greatest attractions of the area now.

How to get there

Orford Ness and the surrounding area has long been a magnet for walkers: W. G. Sebald's hypnotic fictional memoir The Rings of Saturn, *plus the walking histories by Robert Macfarlane, have only sharpened that appetite. So you will not be alone! However, the National Trust-run Orford Ness nature reserve is only open in the summer months, from April through to October. A ferry service sails to the shingle spit. To drive to Orford, the village lies 12 miles east of the A12, on the B1095. The nearest railway station, Wickham Market, is eight miles away.*

SECRET SUBURBS

The Nuclear Terminus and
the Soviet Spy

Euston Street, London NW1

Just a little to the west of Euston station, in a complex of buildings that look from the outside like ordinary offices, there were once men who sought to harness the very building blocks of matter and bend them to their will. They were not mad scientists. Rather the reverse. They were cool-headed engineers and physicists who, for the most part, were engaged in the sort of work that might make others yawn a little. Yet at the core of this institution was a wartime secret so grave that its repercussions would cast a long shadow not only over the Second World War, but over the Cold War that followed as well.

What was more extraordinary was that this secret was uncovered by a young woman who herself was concealing her true allegiances. A woman who lived in the most spruce and perfect corner of suburbia, who, by her actions, helped to shift the geopolitical balance of power between mighty governments. The buildings that this drama slowly unfolded in are still there, in a slightly dusty back street that few would ever walk down by chance. There is no clue now – and nor was there in the 1930s and 1940s – that the future of the world was being changed from within.

The institute in question was the British Non-Ferrous Metals Research Association (BNFMRA), the sort of dry-as-dust name you might find in a comic novel if the hero was working somewhere especially boring. It had been set up in 1920 and was there primarily for any industries working with copper, zinc, lead and other metals and alloys. But there was always more going on here than just large factory owners and corporations seeking out new ways to use metals. Here was scientific research that would always have value beyond the work gates. For instance, there was careful experimentation to do with corrosion which was beyond valuable for pipes and pump works, especially any that might be used in a defensive capacity. In the 1930s, there was a constant awareness that war could come again. In 1939, the BNFMRA gained a spruce new set of offices and laboratories, now spanning a greater area of that Euston back-street and the space behind, and faced in an elegant Art Deco style.

Through the main doors was a maze of laboratories, foundries, a grand library and a great boardroom. The heavier equipment was sited down in the basement, and in the higher stories were physics labs. On the ground floor were high-ceilinged spaces with gantries and pullies with chains, and moving through these spaces were men and women in white coats. There were great numbers of younger people – in fact the institute was recognised as an excellent place to gain experience in anything from 'creep testing' (placing certain materials under loads to measure the pace of strain and stress) to spectography (the analysis of the properties of light). This was where post-graduates left the abstractions of university and saw how their physics was applied to the wider world. This was a world under the darkening clouds of war. Those non-ferrous metals would soon be needed across landscapes of heavily industrialised conflict.

From the late 1930s, the director was G. L. Bailey, a metallurgist who was to become a valued contributor to ideas for a new kind of conflict. In those recent years, atomic researchers across Europe, from Cambridge to Berlin to Italy, had been making breathtaking leaps forward in science, burrowing deep down into the structure of matter to try to achieve fission. Could this be a viable source of almost unlimited energy? And could this be fashioned into a weapon that the world had never before imagined?

As the war went on, G. L. Bailey was inducted into one of its most confidential trajectories: the race for atomic weaponry. It was known that the Nazis had been pushing hard in that direction and their lack of success was ironically partly because of their demonic persecution of the Jews. Berlin's most famous physicist – Albert Einstein – had emigrated at the dawn of Hitler's reign. Other scientists were side-lined or hounded. The Nazis refused to countenance any astounding discoveries made by Jewish scientists because they genuinely believed that such discoveries would either be wrong or deliberately mendacious.

Meanwhile, among the Allies, the gravity of war was taking scientists deep into the deserts of Los Alamos, New Mexico, for work on The Manhattan Project, the aim of which was to produce the first atomic bomb. There was a great deal of collaboration between American and British scientists. And among those whose very specific expertise was consulted was G. L. Bailey. While British Non-Ferrous Metals personnel were looking into the possibilities of nuclear energy, their director was privy to a rather darker purpose.

And it was into this institute in 1937 that a young clerk/secretary came to work. Melita Norwood – née Sirnis – lived with her chemistry teacher husband Hilary in the airy south-east London suburb of Bexleyheath. This life of semi-detached houses and spacious gardens was, for a great many people in the 1930s, a vision of heaven far from the old leaky terraces and outdoor lavatories of the inner cities. It was unusual though not unheard of for married women to have full-time jobs in that era. But Mrs Norwood, who was in her mid-twenties, was a most attentive employee.

She and her husband were also unusual in the sense that they both shared an uncompromising belief in Communism, and in the Soviet Union. Melita Norwood – whose Latvian father and English mother were also deeply immersed in the far left – had originally been a member of the Independent Labour Party, but it was not enough. She had a zeal for the Russian vision of socialism and yearned to do all that she could to help.

Agent Hola:
Melita Norwood,
civil servant and spy
for the KGB. Photo
about 1935.

In 1943, she left the institute to have a baby, but by the following year, she had returned and was working full-time for Bailey. In 1944, the work of the atomic scientists was nearing fruition. And Bailey was receiving technical updates which were labelled under the bland-sounding cover of 'Tube Alloys'. No potential spy would surely take any interest in something as quotidian as metal reports?

But Melita Norwood did, not because she was a highly trained scientist (she wasn't) but because she was voraciously on the lookout for interesting-looking and secret material. Bailey was always careful about placing Tube Alloys documentations in his two safes, one in the office and one in his London home. Given the sensitivity surrounding British Non-Ferrous Metals, each staff member now had to be vetted by MI5. Despite her intense Communist leanings, Melita Norwood passed the vetting and Bailey grew to trust her. What no one knew was that by this stage, she had a Soviet handler in London. She also had her own code name: 'Hola'. She had been provided with a special spy camera and she was spending her evenings obtaining copies of documents from her place of work to pass on to her handler, and thereafter to the scientists of the Soviet Union.

'Hola' did not have the technical knowledge to evaluate the importance of the documents that she was photographing; she didn't have to. The fact that Bailey kept them so carefully hidden away in his safes was indication enough of their importance. At this time, Stalin and his scientists had other informants too. The scientist Klaus Fuchs had been sent from Britain out to Los Alamos to work on the atomic bomb and he had carefully memorised a host of details to pass across. But Melita Norwood was also greatly prized by her Soviet handlers because of the sheer volume of secret information that she managed to smuggle across. It might also be added – generally forgotten in these spy sagas – that even if her conduct was gravely treacherous and reprehensible, it nonetheless took a great deal of bravery.

She was also staggeringly successful: Melita Norwood remained a favourite employee of British Non-Ferrous Metals until 1971. In 1979 – with all her espionage still unsuspected and undiscovered – she took a holiday to Moscow, during which the authorities quietly awarded her the Order of the Red Banner. This came with a cash award too but she turned it down. Melita Norwood had acted as she did because she believed in the Soviet Union. To her, it brought succour and security to the poor, and the goodness it had wrought more than counter-balanced the totalitarian evils that she also acknowledged.

So, it was throughout the war that this curious institution in a drab north London street had seen some of the greatest secrets pass through its doors and its laboratories, and those secrets had been passed in turn directly to an ally that was shortly to become an enemy. Melita Norwood's spying might never have been unearthed were it not for post-Soviet files being opened up, with incredible details of all her years of work. In 1999, she was unmasked to the world. By then, she was 87 years old and devoted to her gardening. The Cold War was a receding memory. She was more an object of amused curiosity than official anger and she was never prosecuted. She came to be dubbed 'The Spy Who Came in From the Co-op'.

As to the building in which one of the greatest espionage coups of the twentieth century was pulled off: it is still there, in a street that remains resolutely overlooked and untidy. But rather than housing laboratories and physics labs, it is now a rather trendy hotel.

HOW TO GET THERE

The site of the former British Non-Ferrous Metals Research Association in Euston Street is not very much more than a few steps to the west of Euston station railway terminus, which is also on the Northern and Victoria Line. Another nearby tube station is Euston Square, on the Circle and Hammersmith and City Lines.

The Nazi Invasion of Birmingham

Wrentham, Gooch and Essex Street, Birmingham

The Luftwaffe had smashed their way through. Houses were left roofless, or simply sliced in half; parlours and bedrooms were now exposed to the world. This was the residential area of the busy industrial hub of Birmingham that had been bombed beyond repair. And yet in and around those ruins, fighting went on. Away from curious eyes, and in conditions of some confidentiality, roads that had once been filled with playing children were now stalked by grim-jawed men with an array of weaponry. Above some doors could be seen the insignia of the Nazi eagle and in one street, there stood a tank with German markings. And some of the men who moved stealthily through this twilit rubble were wearing German uniforms. This was the invasion of Britain by the Wehrmacht.

It wasn't, of course. But the truth was no less intriguing and indeed revealing. These streets were blocked off and taken over by the Home Guard, which is now indelibly associated with the gentle, affectionate comedy of *Dad's Army*. The area was intended for a purpose that it would be difficult to envisage Corporal Jones accepting with equanimity. This was where platoons were taught to kill in street-by-street fighting and taught to square up to the enemy not on the battlefield but face to face among familiar houses and shops, tangled with defensive barbed wire. There was no whimsy about any of this; the Birmingham Home Guard Street Fighting School was commanded by men who were lethally serious.

The Chief Instructor was Captain Edwards, who had served with the Royal Leicester Regiment since 1919. The area in which his specialised training took place was in the area of Wrentham Street, Gooch Street and Essex Street. After the Blitz of 1940, it was a haunting stretch of wilderness – as well as all the naked roof rafters, the collapsed brickwork and the shattered glass, there were open patches of wasteland and the square shape of a water storage reservoir at the centre, dug out especially for the city's firefighters to use. Yet this bleak prospect was turned to lively purpose (as chronicled marvellously now in archival form on staffshomeguard.co.uk) and Home Guard platoons from up and down the country were brought here for short – and very intensive – training sessions.

The day would open with a technical lecture about 'town fighting' and its 'characteristics'. There was an exercise called 'Penetration Demonstration' and a short course in 'crossing obstacles'. There was a tour of the training area, and a lecture simply entitled: 'Defence'. Then, over several days, the programme would intensify. The men – middle-aged or very young – would learn the art of 'concealment' and the techniques of using artillery in residential streets. They were taught how to launch attacks on houses and those who were hidden within. They were taught how to take that house over and 'prepare it for defence' with an array of deadly weaponry. They were taught about booby-traps and about impeding the progress of tanks. There was also – rather wonderfully – a short instructive play, which began with the opening premise that the country had been invaded by the enemy forty-eight hours earlier, and that in all cities, fighting was being conducted house to house.

In this play, a private has seen some of the enemy entering a house on Russell Street and so he races to inform his immediate superior. The house is identified as belonging to the local fishmonger. The first moves are to get armed men into observation positions on nearby roofs, their faces are to be blacked up and all 'papers and coins' are to be removed from their pockets. Having established that there are five enemy soldiers in the house, an attacking platoon is issued with guns and grenades. The aim, simply, is to 'destroy' them, though it is stressed that they should also endeavour to bring back one prisoner alive. Number two rifleman will be responsible for 'killing the man on the roof'; the plan is for the attacking Home Guard to go in via the top and make their way down through the house, eliminating the foe. Any 'boche' running out of the front door are to be shot.

The operation is broadly a success, though one of the Home Guard is killed in the battle, and another is wounded. The men succeed in taking their prisoner and bringing him back to HQ, where he refuses to answer questions. He is hauled off stage with the words 'come on, you blighter' ringing in his ears. And the curtain comes down just as the telephone rings alerting the platoon to 'fifth columnists' flashing torches on roofs.

All this was taking place in 1943 when at the cinemas, 'The Life and Death of Colonel Blimp' opened with a scene involving troops staging an invasion of London, and Colonel Blimp's Home Guard under orders to thwart it (the troops sneakily attack early, leading Blimp to cry 'but war starts at midnight!'). The truth was that invasion in real life was a fantastically remote possibility at that stage in the war. Nonetheless, the Home Guard were determined that even the most unlikely contingency should be planned for. And in Birmingham, these ghostly streets, this panorama of silent wet rubble, were powerfully suggestive of an alternative reality. The cunning street dressings aided the illusion along with the bountiful amount of captured German equipment that was used to dress this outdoor stage.

Even in 1944, the training sessions were going on and curiously, not long after in Germany, the Nazi equivalent of the Home Guard – the Volkssturm – was also being prepared for street fighting. The Red Army was closing in on Germany fast. And the reality of house-to-house fighting, as the citizens of Berlin saw, was deathly and apocalyptic. In Birmingham, even the deadly training had a note of human optimism about it. In Germany, the civilians over whose lives the Nazis ruled, were at last forced to see the true obscenity of war close up.

In common with many cities, it took some years before restoration could come and the ideology of 1950s and 1960s architects held the city of Birmingham in a concrete dual-carriageway vice for years after that. But now, the little area around Wrentham Street and Gooch Street that played host to brilliantly enthusiastic Home Guard men has gone through a thorough transformation. The area, just a little to the south of Birmingham New Street station, now lies within Gay Village, and boasts some plush luxury apartments.

How to get there

Wrentham and Essex Streets are quite close – about twenty minutes' walk or so – immediately south of Birmingham New Street railway station and Birmingham city centre.

Chocolates and Explosives

Rowntree's confectionary factory, York

Imagine the circumstances where the demands of your secret war work could result in your hair turning bright orange. This was the case in what was a vast Rowntree's chocolate factory.

Where once had been production lines filled with minty chewing gum, processing towards wrapping, were now conveyor belts of bomb parts. Women in headscarves focused hard upon their new tasks. Where once they had been working to satisfy the nation's sweet tooth, they were now contributing to the war effort, and all without telling family or friends what it was that they were now doing. They were bound by total secrecy.

There were some aspects of war production – aeroplane factories for instance – that were simply too large to be disguised. When it came to the manufacture of vital weaponry components, though, the work could be cloaked. This not only to protect it from attacks by German bombers; the precautions were there because of the ever-present fear of spies. The proud and historic city of York, with its rich architectural heritage, was a vulnerable target as it was. So, the women who trooped through the gates of the Rowntree's chocolate factory a little to the north of the city hardly needed to be told that their work was seriously confidential.

One such worker was Mary Storey-Richmond, who kept her role so quiet that even years after the war, her family were still a little hazy about what went on in those works. Her niece Mary Broadhead recalled that they had hints that she worked with 'some kind of explosive'. 'She used to say that they had to put their hands inside boxes to do whatever it was that they were doing. I think she mentioned the word "cordite". They had to be very careful. In fact, there were one or two bangs – but she always said nobody was seriously hurt.'[8]

These things are relative as another worker, Florence Clark, recalled that one of her colleagues 'had her fingers blown off.'[9] This in itself, though horrible, was not surprising, considering some of the items on those production lines involved fuses made for shells for 25lb guns, filled with TNT, and anti-tank mine fuses. The work was extraordinarily concentrated and twelve-hour shifts on those unrelenting wartime production lines were not uncommon. The atmosphere on the floor was watchful and careful, for there was explosive everywhere. Naturally, smoking was forbidden (as indeed it had been through the years of bountiful chocolate production) but there were other more unusual strictures too. There were rooms for the application of special make-up, to afford some skin protection. Refreshment came in the form of cold

Handle with care: munitions work, County Industries, York, 1943.

milk, rather than tea or coffee (to avoid electrics such as kettles near the production lines). And the women all had to wear turbans. Any loose hair that protruded would, over the course of a twelve-hour shift, turn either bright orange or bright yellow. The workers 'were called the canaries', said Mary Broadhead.[10]

Indeed, Florence Clark remembered that the TNT could not only affect hair, but also skin. Before the make-up was introduced, there were those whose faces and arms turned lemon yellow and occasionally even the soles of their feet. In effect, their bodies had been exposed to poison, and no one at the time was making a study of long-term effects.

Given the intense technicality and jeopardy of the work, it now seems also remarkable that the supervising managers were the same chocolate and sweet executives who, before the war, oversaw the production of Fruit Gums. The director was George Spencer Crossley and N. G. Sparkes was the works manager. They looked to Royal Ordnance works for their inspiration in turning spearmint chewing gum production lines into this extraordinarily delicate operation. But this is still not quite as remarkable as those hundreds of women who accepted the dangers and the difficulties to turn their hands from sweets to high explosives. They did their bit with valour but also without any acclaim. For some, the secrecy held – as sometimes happened after the war, if no precise instructions were issued about what it was now permissible to talk about, the women assumed that the confidentiality was still iron.

As to the sweets, war brought the inevitable privations of rationing and indeed it was only some years after the conflict that the public could once more enjoy the full gamut of soft-centred milk chocolates to the sweet rasp of Fruit Pastilles. And still those production-line women could not explain exactly why their hair had changed in such an extraordinary way.

HOW TO GET THERE

Although many of the old chocolate factory sites have been closed pending redevelopment – for a while they became the haunt of urban explorers, taking atmospheric photographs of abandoned factory floors – the sites can still be seen a mile or so north of the city centre, in the Clifton area on Haxby Road. But more on the history of Rowntree's can be found all over the city, which prides itself on a heritage of chocolate and sweets. There is in fact a dedicated chocolate museum. Thus, any visit will be suffused with sweet-toothed sensations, with the advantage that none will turn your hair bright orange. York is about twenty minutes from the M1 and there is a regular park and ride service into the city centre. York railway station is a busy junction on the East Coast Line, with express routes to Edinburgh and London.

Cryptographers in Prison

Wormwood Scrubs prison, London W12

The architecture of Wormwood Scrubs prison has a markedly forbidding feel – with high brick walls, unornamented prospects of dark brown, and narrow, almost medieval, windows, it was intended to cast a chill on any soul who had the misfortune of being sent there. To the building's north lay a large boggy expanse of open ground, eventually curtailed by a busy railway line. Even for the innocent people who lived close by to this edifice, it was never a prospect that could cheer a day, particularly since their own tenement buildings and houses seemed just as severe. All in all, it was a most unlikely location for a fox-hunting Oxford don to burrow his way into the Nazi secret service.

Wormwood Scrubs prison is positioned to the industrial west of London, in the suburb of Acton, close to a vast area of busy factories and breweries. Built in the late nineteenth century, this substantial and grim edifice was arranged around different blocks, each as spartan as the other. Even up to the outbreak of the Second World War, the prison regime was gruelling, with tough manual labour and food rations that frequently left prisoners hungry by the end of the day. This was a prospect of green-tiled cells, high barred windows, and the constant clangour of iron walkways.

But the oncoming conflict and the certainty that the Nazi war machine would launch devastating bomb attacks at speed meant the authorities had to consider what to do with the establishment. Lying so close as it did to potential heavy industrial targets – power stations as well as large manufacturing plants – it would almost certainly be bombed as well. So, the idea was that the prisoners should be evacuated to jails further away out of the bomber's direct path. And the newly emptied cells of Block C were turned to new and more ingenious purpose: a top-secret base manned with fine intellects who at the end of the day could leave the prison and return to their billets and shelters.

More than this, Wormwood Scrubs would also be ideally placed and facilitated for securing captured enemy agents. So it was that the young people who came to work here on a daily basis were not remotely put off by their louring surrounds.

The department in question was the Radio Security Service, which itself was an offshoot of MI5. The purpose of the RSS was to monitor the national airwaves for transmissions from spies. Before the war broke out, the department carried out a careful national inventory of all the transmitting radio sets in use, many by gifted radio enthusiasts (of whom we will hear more in another chapter). There was not only concern that spies would use radio technology to beam messages back to their Nazi masters across the Channel, but also that radio transmitters might be deployed to send signals to the skies above, to approaching Luftwaffe bombers who could then fix on them as targets. Naturally, there was an edge of urgency to the radio-oriented work that was set up in the long line of cells in Block C.

A presiding genius of the department was Major Walter Gill who in peacetime was the bursar of Merton College Oxford. It was his distinctive record from the First World War that saw him chosen to manage the department at Wormwood Scrubs, for he had been at the forefront of wireless technology in the Middle East. It was whispered that he had scaled the Great Pyramid itself in order to install a sensitive radio receiver at its peak. Now, in this echoing prison, he worked with a small department of posh young women – debutantes recruited on the grapevines of high society – and technologically minded young men. One notable youthful recruit, however, was rather more owlish and academic. This was the severely bespectacled Hugh Trevor-Roper (later Lord Dacre), a young Oxford don and a historian with a vaulting intellect. The constant clang of the Wormwood Scrubs walkways proved no impediment to the work he carried out in his cell. Trevor-Roper preferred the prison to the drab monotony of the 'council houses' that surrounded it.

He himself had digs in the nearby genteel suburb of Ealing which he also viewed with some disdain. The reason this young man had been deemed unfit for active service was his atrocious eyesight. Though that same eyesight did nothing to stop him gaining some astonishing insights into the inner workings of the Nazi secret service.

As he and Major Gill worked to scour those airwaves for German messages, they hit upon certain frequencies that produced a vast amount of traffic. They were all encoded, naturally, so the transcribed messages initially came out as gibberish. But one night, Trevor-Roper decided (a terrible breach of security, this) to take some work home with him. He walked through the prison gates with a stash of enciphered messages. He took them back to his digs and – during the course of a long luxurious bath – he scrutinised them intensely until finally he fathomed the coded key.

These were messages that had not been properly enciphered by the electric Enigma machine, and as he decoded them, the plain German revealed itself. Trevor-Roper was a fluent speaker of that language. What is more, he had hit an extraordinarily rich seam: these were messages to and from agents of the Abwehr, the Nazi secret service. He and Major Gill thence set to work on their trove, and delightedly let their superiors know what they were achieving. The trouble was that this was quite beyond their remit and what was being unfurled in the incongruous halls of Wormwood Scrubs was an operation that was deemed by others to be a nightmare security risk.

The only people permitted to break high-up German codes were the operatives of the Government Code and

Cypher School. The reason was that the Germans could never be allowed to know that their ciphers had been penetrated because if they ever did find out, they would vastly increase their security and make subsequent coded messages impossible to break. And it was considered that young Trevor-Roper, blithely reading Abwehr messages in the bath, was running exactly that kind of risk. His and Gill's superiors wanted them to stop. But having hit such a rich vein of intelligence – chatter directly from the heart of the Nazi secret service – they could not bear to leave such work.

They were made to. Perhaps there was an element of inter-departmental rivalry with the official codebreakers jealously holding close their brilliant work. But the situation was serious enough for the director of Bletchley Park, Alistair Denniston, to pay a jittery visit to Wormwood Scrubs prison. He went with one of his senior cryptographers, Oliver Strachey. Trevor-Roper and Major Gill, although under orders to desist, did receive a small accolade as Strachey set up a special department at Bletchley Park to devote itself to the Abwehr output that they had established a hook into.

Not that this was quite the end, for within those tiled cells, Major Gill and Trevor-Roper continued to pick up Abwehr transmissions – all part of their remit – and could not resist going on to crack four more sets of ciphers. Nor was this the end of Trevor-Roper's association with Bletchley Park and as one of the very few people in the country permitted to know what was actually happening up at that Buckinghamshire estate (as we will see in a later chapter), he always made the most of his visits into the countryside near the Park, and he rode with the nearby Whaddon Hunt.

Meanwhile, the debutantes and radio geniuses were not destined to stay in their Wormwood Scrubs cells for long. It was becoming clearer that a direct hit in the Blitz seemed inevitable. As we shall see in the following chapter, a new home was found for the Radio Security Service – at the very heart of suburban respectability.

How to get there

Obviously, a tour of C Block is rather out of the question, no matter how pure the historical motives. Those cells remain fully occupied to this day. However, to get a taste of what the code-breakers saw day by day, the severe exterior of the prison and the bleak expanse of Wormwood Scrubs at its northern end are worth a bracing walk. The prison is on Du Cane Road and the nearest tube station is East Acton (Central Line). The number 7 bus route winds its leisurely way into central London.

The Schoolboy Spooks

Arkley View, Arkley, near Chipping Barnet, Herts

Hunched over the glowing tuner of the receiver, head-phones in place, in the front parlour in his parents' house in Tooting Bec, was bona fide secret operative, seventeen-year-old Ray Fautley. For him, this was the stuff of adventure-story daydreams come true. He was working under conditions of the strictest secrecy, having had a visit from a Man From The Ministry. None of his friends could know, even though it would have brought him the greatest glory to tell them. Even Ray's parents – who dutifully relegated themselves to the back room on those intense evenings – had no real idea what their son was working on. Nor indeed did his girlfriend Barbara. This would soon create a crisis for the young secret agent. But the fact was that he, along with some 1,500 other people, very young and very old, up and down the country, were involved in properly serious work. They formed the threads of a web which all led back to a rather nice villa at the northernmost tip of London, just a short distance from High Barnet. It was called Arkley View. Many of those who worked for it, such as young

Ray Fautley, knew it better by the stark postal address: PO Box 25, Barnet.

Ray was a Voluntary Interceptor. His role was to find and focus on German radio operators and the messages that they sent out into the field. He had to combine this secret activity with Home Guard duties, plus his full-time job, which just happened to be with a specialised south London radio components company. Since his early boyhood, Ray had been mesmerised by radio technology. He started work full time at fourteen at Marconi and it was there that some older colleagues taught him Morse code. Ray was extremely proficient and fast at translating and transcribing it, and when war came, it was his colleagues who ensured that the relevant authorities knew of his expertise.

Some Voluntary Interceptors were recruited via their membership of The Radio Society of Great Britain, which told the authorities who had the skills and the licensed equipment. Others, youths like Ray, were sought out because high-speed Morse needed young brains. It was frazzling work tuning in to enemy frequencies and transcribing every last 'dit dit dot' with 100 per cent accuracy.

That said, the moment that Ray found himself inducted into a new secret world was almost comically clichéd. One evening, as he and his parents were finishing their supper, a visitor materialised on their Tooting doorstep: a man in a suit, bowler hat and holding an umbrella. He asked specifically to come in to talk to young Ray, with the parents out of the room. Naturally, this caused consternation in son and parents alike.

'There was this chap in a bowler, with an umbrella, he was doing background on me,' said Mr Fautley decades later. 'Asking me where my parents were born; where my grandparents were born. Most were from London. None came from further than the Isle of Wight. When this Voluntary Interceptor gentleman, with his bowler and umbrella, was leaving, I said to him, "Would you please say a few words to my parents?" I said, "They'll think I've done something awful and that I'm going to be taken away and locked up." The man said, "All right" and within my hearing, he said to my parents: "Your son will be doing work of very great national importance to this country." I thought, what on earth . . .'[11]

Young Ray needed specialist equipment, and so a vast and unwieldy AR88 radio receiver was delivered. The idea was that it should be hidden within a bureau in the front parlour. There were other items, including specially printed notepads, and envelopes marked in bright red with the word 'SECRET'. He would be scanning suggested frequencies, and within time, he would be fixing on individual German operators (even with something like Morse code, the sender of messages always had an individual, distinctive style). These were messages to and from the Nazi secret service, the Abwehr. Many of its operators prefaced coded messages with predictable greetings such as 'Heil Hitler' that could be used as clues for decryption. They were much more talkative through Morse than any of their British counterparts. And they sometimes told each other of forthcoming code changes; all of which was golden intelligence to the codebreakers at Bletchley Park.

Ray would be secretly listening in for two hours every evening, five days a week. His logbooks, filled with transcribed messages, would then be sent on to that mysterious PO Box in leafy High Barnet. Given the intense secrecy, he was never allowed to know precisely what valuable intelligence he had gathered. But frequently, young Ray would receive letters of thanks from the team at Arkley View for the excellence of his work.

Indeed, the base at Arkley View was something of a secret interception cottage industry. As well as the handsome villa, there were huts dotted around the wooded surrounds, in which radio experts would be billeted. Arkley and close-by Barnet were set high on the hills above London and on clear days, it was possible to see right across the valley of the Thames to the hills in the south. All of which of course was advantageous for radio aerials. The recruitment of Voluntary Interceptors was powered by the initiative of Lord Sandhurst who was co-ordinating their efforts. He was a man who liked to communicate his enthusiasm and good humour (he sent out newsletters to his recruits in which he would refer to himself as 'T. W. Earp.'). Sandhurst was running a junior Bletchley-style operation. Arkley itself was a very small village, and next-door Barnet was a scarcely much larger suburb. And so it created little in the way of local curiosity.

It was also something of a sanctuary for Hugh Trevor-Roper, mentioned before in the Wormwood Scrubs chapter (see 'Cryptographers in Prison', p.112). For his new north London landlady was proving something of a trial whenever he got any time back at home to delve into his classical research. She was pathologically talkative, and deeply interested in subjects such as: the Lost Realm of Atlantis; the meanings of dreams; the creepy secrets of the Great Pyramid and the nature of the Psychic Dimension. It is possible that all the talk in High Barnet was of little else. But poor Trevor-Roper could not quite summon the strength to deal with this nightly tidal wave of occultist chitter-chatter.

And the work of this branch of the Y Service (the umbrella term that included the Voluntary Interceptors) was providing fascinating material (including secret German messages sent to agents in advance of the 1940 Nazi invasion of France, news of which was pouring through the headphones of radio enthusiasts in ordinary houses up and down the land). There was less news of hostile enemy agents working within England, simply because there were so very few of them. The Radio Security Service, having logged every transmitter in the country, was hyper-alert to the possibility of rogue elements getting intelligence out of the country. Indeed, later on in the war, there were such agents – but they were not Nazis. There were Communist sympathisers (at a time when of course Britain was an ally of the Soviet Union) such as Ursula Beurton, who lived in Oxfordshire near the Rollright Stones and had a secret transmitter which she concealed within the stone wall of her back garden.

But for the Voluntary Interceptors, the work was about the quiet, secret satisfaction that they were carrying out a vital role in the war effort. The teenage Ray Fautley, monitoring the airwaves in that Tooting front parlour, encountered the curious phenomenon of 'getting to know' individual German operators, and like Fautley, they were young. However, unlike him, they were prone to sending unguarded language and jocular obscenities to their fellow German operators. Their personalities somehow emerged from that fog of Morse. Sometimes the vulgar banter would be used as they set up that day's codes and the bad language would be used by the codebreakers as a further lever into the codes of the hapless Abwehr.

The secrecy of the work was not always ideal though; because of the demanding hours, Ray had to tell his girl-friend Barbara that he could only now see her on Saturday nights and that their usual Wednesday assignations were now off. He would be at home but she was forbidden to come knocking. Unfortunately, he could not tell her why. And it was possible that a seething jealous suspicion built up in Barbara's mind from that point. Whatever the case, she was driven to a state of boiling indignation and, one Wednesday, together with a girlfriend, she marched round to Ray's house and demanded entry. The teenager's parents gingerly opened the front door and tried to explain to Barbara that while Ray was at home, he couldn't possibly see her.

With that, she marched past them, opened the door of the front parlour – and beheld her boyfriend hunched over the intricate-looking radio equipment, headphones on. Barbara's instant (and rather disloyal) assumption was that her boyfriend was a Nazi spy. Without a word, she turned and ran off into the street. Ray, terrified that she would be looking for a policeman, gave chase. He eventually caught up with her and managed as best he could – without disclosing the nature of the work – to tell her that his radio expertise had led to a visit from the Man From The Ministry. Barbara not only happily accepted this, but not long after went on to marry Ray, and they were together for many decades afterwards.

How to get there

Arkley View – the house itself – is regretfully long gone. But the area is still worth visiting to get a flavour of the milieu that young thunderbolts like Hugh Trevor-Roper operated from. The commuter village of Arkley lies about a mile west from the busy shopping streets of Barnet. As a bonus historical point, just a little to the north of those shopping streets lies a lovely wooded common which, in 1471, was the site of one of the bloody battles in the Wars of the Roses. The area is served by a tube terminus, High Barnet (Northern Line).

The Crafty Cockney on the Hill

The GPO Research Laboratories, Dollis Hill,
London NW10

We somehow expect world-changing events to happen in extraordinary places, like the development of the atom bomb in the eerie deserts of Los Alamos, for instance. Yet the advent of the computer – a far more seismic revolution – partly happened on top of a hill overlooking 1930s semi-detached houses and a modest park, in an area with a name that was so strikingly whimsical-sounding that many Londoners wondered if it was even real.

The district was Dollis Hill. The site was a vast 1930s building of brown London brick, looking like a large grammar school, topped with a green clock tower. Yet even as this institute stood in proud view from miles around, the astounding technological leaps made within those walls were among the most ferociously guarded secrets of the war – secrets that would save untold thousands upon thousands of lives.

The Dollis Hill GPO Research Station was instrumental in creating the modern world. The fact that there was also a secret government bunker nearby which was used as an alternative shelter for Winston Churchill and the War Office should Whitehall be engulfed in flame, now seems less pressing.

The other alluring factor in the story of Dollis Hill's finest hour is that it was partly down to serendipity. When it was opened in 1933, the GPO (General Post Office) unit was there to develop new telephone and teleprinter technology and to find ways of speeding up cumbersome systems. The people who worked there were dedicated enthusiasts made up of engineers whose greatest pleasure was working in vast workshops and laboratories on wiring and diodes.

And among them was a man who even early in his career was bending his intellect to the shape of the technological future, a world that went beyond punchcards and telegrams. His achievements would – for many decades – remain the most shadowy of national secrets. Happily, today, that once-anonymous genius now has a road in Dollis Hill named after him.

The engineer in question was Thomas 'Tommy' Flowers. In conjunction with Alan Turing, William Tutte and Gordon Welchman at Bletchley Park, he had been brooding on the ever more advanced codes being used by the Nazis. These codes were generated by electrical machines and in such vast quantities that no human workforce could ever hope to decode and process them all. This was a threat that had to be fought with electronics. And while the Bletchley team had the mathematical genius that could theorise about such an electronic machine

(Alan Turing, who conceived of it in philosophical terms), it was Tommy Flowers who could physically build such a thing and give it proper life. The resulting machines proved an uncanny triumph and, thanks to Flowers, the British could read codes from Hitler's desk.

But the story of how he arrived at this victory within his Dollis Hill laboratories is also one of subliminal class conflict, for there were those who could not believe that a man nicknamed 'the Crafty Cockney' had anywhere near the skill that was needed to build what was in essence the world's first programmable computer.

Flowers' journey to Dollis Hill and the core of Bletchley Park was an unusual tale of social mobility for the time. It started in 1905 in the East End district of Poplar, where he spent his childhood in the shadow of gasworks on the River Lea. His father was a bricklayer, and young Flowers soon developed an intuitive feel for mathematics and engineering. His parents and his teachers could see his talent, and as a teenager he went to East Ham Technical School with a bursary to study mathematics (other youths of his age would have already left school by that point and would be working). From there he joined the vast Royal Arsenal at Woolwich – itself quite an epicentre of secret technology – on an apprenticeship, while at the same time continuing his academic studies in the evening.

In 1926, Flowers joined the General Post Office, which was not merely concerned with the delivery of letters, but also very much involved in the nation's nascent telephone network, as well as telegrams and radio transmissions. Now the young man completed his studies at the University of London while spending his days looking at the new electrical possibilities for dramatically expanding and improving telecommunications. By the time he arrived at the new Dollis Hill laboratories, he was already thinking about ideas for electronics, an entirely new field, as revolutionary as the later microchips.

Back then, anyone making a telephone call had to be routed through a human operator and Flowers was preoccupied with modernising the system so that a person might simply dial a number and get straight through. Such ideas were then futuristic.

And as the thunderous clouds of war gathered over the vast city, Flowers soon found himself drawn into the most carefully guarded of all the nation's secrets: the fight to crack the Nazi codes. At Bletchley Park, the brilliant young don Gordon Welchman, together with resident genius Alan Turing, had devised a vast wardrobe-sized machine called the Bombe, which was designed to work its way through the thousands of different potential code combinations found in intercepted messages.

Alan Turing, of course, had for some years been applying both mathematical and philosophical reasoning to the creation of a machine that could think. When he wanted a technical modification made to the Bombe, it was Tommy Flowers that he consulted, and so impressed was Turing with the GPO scientist that he bore him in mind for all future technical challenges at Bletchley.

In 1943, that expertise was required when the Nazis sharpened up their own technology and brought in a whizz-bang new encryption process. Flowers and a Dollis Hill colleague, together with the theoretical expertise of Bletchley's Professor Max Newman and Bill Tutte, came up with their first response. It was a code-reading contraption of wires and spools and tapes that came to be known as the 'Heath Robinson' because it looked like one of the mad inventions illustrated by that famous comic artist.

But it was Flowers who began to see how an improved machine could also be made less temperamental. It was all down to thermionic valves. Again, with Professor Newman, Flowers set to work taking his creation off the draughtsman's page and into the world.

Naturally, this meant that the already tight secrecy around the Dollis Hill workshops was increased extensively. Though as Tommy Flowers' son Kenneth recalled many years later, there was a tiny exception: men were permitted to tell their wives simply that they were engaged in confidential work. This was for the maintenance of marital harmony. Otherwise, long unexplained hours at the research institute and constantly arriving home late might give rise to suspicions of an affair.

Indeed, although everyone at the Dollis Hill base was rather too busy at the height of the war to consider such things, there were, for the time, an unusual number of women working there. And when it came to the creation of Colossus in 1944, Tommy Flowers had a team of male and female engineers set to bring his vision to life.

It was to be a programmable, super-fast machine that could power its way through thousands of combinations, made up of one length of tape, fewer spools, a wall of flashing lights and switches and thrumming with the power of thousands of thermionic valves. However, the general scepticism felt by Gordon Welchman about this non-Oxbridge East End man, combined with more general scarcity of wartime resources, meant that Flowers had a struggle finding the parts to assemble the Colossus. He paid for many out of his own pocket, such was his commitment to realising this vision.

And the machine proved to be a marvel. If it was kept switched on constantly, it did not cut out or break down, which was a fantastic boon when codes had to be read during crisis. And it worked with such smooth speed that it became possible for the codebreakers to read Nazi messages almost in real time, with very little delay. Ten Colossi were made and remained in operation right until the very end of the war – and beyond. For what were termed security reasons, eight of the machines were dismantled come the 1945 victory, but two were retained and spirited away to the newly regenerated Government Communications Headquarters.

And the post-war secrecy meant that the world could not know the full weight of what had been achieved in that workshop on a north London hilltop: they weren't to know that Tommy Flowers had opened the door to a new computer age. Professor Max Newman, who had been central to the Colossus project, went on with Alan Turing

*The genius who
changed the future:
Tommy Flowers.*

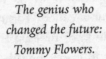

to teach at Manchester University where they continued the quest to develop a more broadly functioning computer. Thomas Flowers, meanwhile, received an award of £1,000 from the government, which just about reimbursed him for his own personal investment in Colossus. He was awarded an OBE (though the reason for it could not be cited).

He realised the potential of what he had achieved at Dollis Hill, and after the war he was very keen to explore further the possibility of bringing new computers into the world. But a combination of official secrecy and establishment inertia thwarted that ambition. Nonetheless, he stayed with the GPO. And he went on to invent ERNIE, the computer used for premium bond prizes.

When at last the veil of confidentiality was lifted from the Bletchley story in the 1980s, Tommy Flowers became a much-feted hero of the wider computing community with his contribution at last given its proper recognition. Now, the Dollis Hill laboratories have been converted into hilltop flats but his legacy has not been forgotten. The road leading into the development is now called 'Tommy Flowers Close'. Elsewhere, in the little knot of East End streets where he was brought up there is, upon the side of a slightly crumbling 1950s shopping parade, a huge wall mosaic of Flowers' bespectacled face bearing a slightly enigmatic smile. There is also a pop-up pub/art space on this site that is named, appropriately, 'The Tommy Flowers'. His younger self might have smiled even more enigmatically at the tribute.

How to get there

The building that once housed this most extraordinary wartime secret still dominates the skyline in this corner of north London suburbia, from the south and the north. To reach it involves (for urban types) something of a climb. The most pleasing route is through Dollis Hill Park, and past Dollis Hill House. The nearest tube station is Dollis Hill (Jubilee Line) although Neasden (also Jubilee Line) is very roughly the same distance too. As mentioned, there are no laboratories now, instead, there are swanky apartments overlooking the city. But the site has a pleasingly offbeat historical resonance, nonetheless.

Super-Spies in Pinstripes

RAF Eastcote, Middlesex

As the computer revolution got underway in Dollis Hill, the earlier prototype machines that had fuelled it were chuntering away all day and throughout the night just several miles to the west, in a vast secret codebreaking factory in the heart of prosperous commuterland. The women who tended to these monsters were stoic, for the work was exacting, and the machines were prone to temper tantrums. Patience was also a necessity when it came to the canteen food.

Eastcote was (and is) a community of Tudorbethan semi-detached houses linked to inner London by a tube station on the Piccadilly and Metropolitan lines. In the middle of the twentieth century, this was a well-to-do district of bank managers and financial brokers and in their midst was an establishment that any Nazi spy would have given his back teeth to learn about.

The surrounding wire fence and the clumps of trees partially obscured what was in any case a rather drab view. This was a complex comprising very long, high concrete buildings with notably slender windows positioned high up in the walls. RAF Eastcote was very obviously contributing to the war effort. But none of its neighbours could have begun to have guessed quite how.

In essence, this was the factory floor of Bletchley Park. Up in Buckinghamshire, the theoretical calculations for drilling into those codes were being performed in make-do huts. In Eastcote, the machines – 'bombes' – dreamed up by Alan Turing and Gordon Welchman were going about their 'clicking, ticking' business (the noise they made, said veteran Jean Valentine, was like noisy knitting[12]). The size of wardrobes, they were fitted with rows of rotating drums, their edges inscribed with letters. Round the back of these contraptions were intricate mazes of wiring. They were the very devil to maintain. But the work that they were advancing through – each machine in each bay allocated its own region on earth, from Greece to Vladivostock – meant that the codebreakers were achieving breakthroughs on an industrial scale. The messages being relayed back from every part of the globe were being processed here and turned into crystalline intelligence.

And the Eastcote site was to remain core to the business of cryptography some time after the end of the war too. It was to become the first headquarters of GCHQ. All in all, throughout the course of the war years, some several thousand personnel, the majority of whom were women, were based here. If the locals ever wondered what was going on, they were polite enough never to ask. But for some of the women who worked at Eastcote, here was a place in history, even if they were not to know

Slaves to the machines: Wrens overseeing the revolutionary code-unravelling Bombe machines at the secret base in Eastcote.

it at the time; in fact, they were helping to harness the tides of war.

One such recruit was Ruth Bourne, who had excelled at languages at school. She had been offered a place at the University of London, but the war made it impossible for her to think of taking it up: she felt she had to do her bit. And so she volunteered for the Women's Royal Naval Service. Perhaps it was her skill with French, German and Spanish that led the authorities to spot her. With another Wrens recruit, Jean Valentine, the crucial attribute was an addiction to cryptic crossword puzzles. In the cases of both these young women, they were sent along with other Wrens for initial general naval training at a castle in Scotland called Tullichewan and not long after they found themselves called to one side to be told that they had been selected for 'Special Duties X'.

Some went to Bletchley; some found themselves being posted to secret out-stations around the world. Jean Valentine, aged just nineteen, was sent to Colombo in Ceylon (now Sri Lanka) where she spent her nights intercepting coded messages in bamboo huts while fighting off the local tropical wildlife. Others came to Eastcote which, while having little that was glamorous about it and certainly not the great weather of Sri Lanka, did at least mean that off-duty hours could be spent at dances in central London. Escapism was sorely needed as the work was very intense. Wrens had to stand watch over the Bombe machines and instantly report to more senior figures when the machines reached a 'stop', that is, had successfully unravelled a particular code. But the machines broke down often as well, with the wiring around the back having to be constantly adjusted with tweezers. And the furious concentration could also prove a mental strain, quite frequently there were instances where the Wren operators rather than their machines would break down. The remedy? Half a day in bed with a jug of orange squash on the bedside table.

The canteen was regarded by some with horror. One Wren recalled an apparent speciality of 'liver floating in water'.[13] Yet there was a sense of community here too. Also posted to the station were male RAF mechanics and some 150 American military codebreakers, billeted nearby in a barracks at Ruislip Woods. This meant that as well as the night-life that lay directly on the Piccadilly Line into the West End, there were also home-grown entertainments; Wrens and other personnel put on plays. In August 1944, a production of *Ladies In Retirement*, a work set in an old house on the Thames Estuary in the late Victorian era, was staged at the Pinner County School. The amateur thespians and stagehands threw their all into these shows. The programme for this production included credits for both lighting and sound effects.

There was sport too, including a furiously competitive hockey team. Another advantage of Eastcote was that it lay close to some superb open countryside, meaning that summertime cricket fixtures and other games were conducted amid rich fields and dappled meadows. By the end of the war, when the time came for the young Wrens to be demobilised and returned to their former lives, there were some pangs of unexpected regret. An affectionate and humorous poem and an ode to the base and the Bombe machines was composed by 'H. Newton' and 'C. Campbell' in memory:

> I must go back to Eastcote again
> To the busy bays and the laughter
> And all I ask is an EVENING WATCH
> With thoughts of sleep soon after
> And the wheels' click and the motors' song
> And the typewriters chattering
> And the thankful look on everyone's face
> When 'tea boat' comes clattering.[14]

But this was not the end of the base. As the war ended, and as Bletchley Park was cleared out, there was still a most urgent and pressing need for codebreakers when the world entered a new era of Cold War diplomacy, and the two great blocs of Soviet Russia and America started to clash. Though the Wrens dispersed, a number of the experienced Bletchley codebreakers – several of whom had been with the Government Code and Cypher School since the First World War – now found themselves among the Eastcote pin-striped commuters, although travelling in the opposite direction. Bletchley was regenerating into GCHQ, and before it moved to its new home of Cheltenham (where it is still sited today), it was originally in Eastcote where the Secret Listeners squared up to the neuroses of the Nuclear Age. Some things remained constant; there was cricket (ace codebreaker Hugh Alexander was less consistent near the stumps though did not lack for enthusiasm) and indeed tutorials on Highland dancing (the speciality of Hugh Foss). By 1952, this most secret of departments was spirited away, though the base remained, part concealed within those charming woods. Only relatively recently has the site been claimed by the ubiquitous 'luxury housing' estate.

HOW TO GET THERE

Even though the base no longer exists, and even though the housing that now stands in its place is in every way unremarkable, Eastcote is worth a visit for every cryptology enthusiast because it is so very easy to imagine, when you get there, what it was like back in the 1940s. You leave the underground station, turn north, and head upwards past a shopping parade that would, back then, have comprised grocers, butchers, banks and haberdashery shops. And a little further on from this are little greens and a pretty nineteenth-century church and some fine examples of sleek 1930s residential architecture. The cryptologists were very much part of this world but the local pubs in those days would have had a more distinctly rural flavour. Eastcote sits on the tube lines of Piccadilly (a direct link to the West End) and Metropolitan (a faster service pointing towards the City).

The Camberwell Eavesdroppers

Metropolitan Police Intercept Station,
Denmark Hill, London SE5

The hills and valleys of south London haunted the imagination of the creator of Sherlock Holmes. Sir Arthur Conan Doyle looked at the large, prosperous suburban villas that nestled in woodland and overlooked the distant spires of the city and he envisaged extraordinary scenes unfolding behind their doors, such as exotic murder or baroque madness. One such house exceeded anything that Holmes might have been able to deduce in real life. From a quiet street on top of a hill that lay close to elegant eighteenth-century terraces, some of the more decisive moves in the secret war were made.

This was an establishment that, from the early 1930s, housed some brilliantly science-fictional-looking technical labs, with equipment that might have been borrowed from the Boris Karloff Frankenstein films. And yet all this top secrecy had the most perfect camouflage. It was housed within a substantial and reassuring redbrick metropolitan police station.

This was an intercept HQ, scanning and monitoring the airwaves, and harvesting vast quantities of encrypted communications. This was a department of 'secret listeners' who came under the umbrella term of 'Y Services'. The 'Y' was just a slang abbreviation of 'wireless'. Among their numbers were radio enthusiasts who were often men and women who were some of the more prominent nerds of their time. But this is not meant to sound unkind, for the obsession that a number of young people had with the developing technology of radio (rather like computer fans today) was to prove utterly invaluable, and not just throughout the war.

Denmark Hill is a well-to-do enclave standing high above Camberwell and looking out northwards towards the glittering Thames and the dome of St Paul's Cathedral. In the early 1930s, a pioneering department moved out from its old offices at Scotland Yard and into more spacious and suitable surrounds amid houses lived in by merchants and writers. The operatives were listening in to radio transmissions. Their focus, before the war, was very tight. They were chiefly intent upon Soviet traffic. In part, this need to gather encrypted communications had been inspired by the General Strike of 1926; might there, the authorities wondered, be more damaging outbreaks of domestic Bolshevism aided and inspired by figures within London's Soviet trade missions?

The man in charge here was Commander Harold Kenworthy. Born in Tottenham, on the opposite side of London, this middle-aged man had already enjoyed an intriguing career. Towards the end of the First World War, he had served in the Royal Navy and had been posted to Gibraltar, where he threw himself into wireless telegraphy work. Come the end of the war, Kenworthy was recruited by the Marconi Wireless Telegraph Company, which was expanding fast across the globe and weaving a web of communication threads between nations and continents. With this infrastructure of cables and masts and the low hum of thermionic valves came fierce interest from the British government in forming some clandestine partnership. Marconi had the means of transmitting messages; the newly formed Government Code and Cypher School had the intense desire to read all the messages that were sent.

This was a brand new age of spying: what previously had to be gleaned by breaking into an ambassador's safe and purloining secret sealed documents – the very idea of which was so ungentlemanly that the government refused – could now be gathered by sitting at a radio receiver with a pair of headphones and a notepad.

The First World War had done away with any ethical flinching. It was simply for the sake of national security that the codebreakers had to be able to monitor the communications of potential future enemies. Britain's empire at that time was still vast. And Commander Kenworthy, now working with Marconi, was sent to India to spread his wireless expertise following the lifting of a ban on private organisations using the technology there.

It transpired that the future Mrs Kenworthy – née Ivy Ford, also of Tottenham – was a devotee of the new age of crystal set transmissions. Back in London by the early 1930s, and living in the busy middle-class suburb of Croydon, Ivy Kenworthy had some of the latest equipment installed in the family home. It was thanks to her experimentation with an undulator – a small, complex electrical box with compact cylinders and ink and paper tape – that she was able to hit on a method of detecting teleprinter transmissions. The undulator was a means of recording machine-sent messages and indeed was the sort of device that would end up being utilised by the codebreakers at Bletchley Park. Commander Kenworthy and Ivy were keen innovators. Indeed, it was Mrs Kenworthy who, when monitoring the undulator one day in 1932, became aware that the automatic tape was showing anomalous traces, 'long lines and little bumps', as she said.[15] These, it was found, were the echoes of foreign teleprinter signals. A few years later, in the grip of conflict, that flash of insight with the undulator was to prove very useful in the efforts to secure a way into Nazi teleprinter message transmissions.

All that was to come. But Commander Kenworthy was one of the figures who was helping to establish the essential framework that was to later help the work of Alan Turing and others. The central interwar codebreaking department, the Government Code and Cypher School, had several branches. It was one thing to decode scrambled secret messages, but where were they to obtain all this miraculous material? Some of the work was delegated to the Metropolitan Police, specifically that of listening closely to the ether for any suggestions of domestic sub-version and foreign (most obviously Russian) interference. The world that we see now had its roots in the techno-logical advances of a century ago.

And under Commander Kenworthy, an impressive establishment was constructed under the cover of that Denmark Hill police station. The rooms housing the ad-vanced radio equipment were futuristic and aesthetically pleasing, all horizontal lines, plenty of light, winking light bulbs, dials and Bakelite. As to the recruits, Commander Kenworthy had his own network of highly eager wireless experts from his naval days. In the 1920s, they cut their teeth seeking out unauthorised radio transmissions in London being sent, it was presumed, by Bolshevik agents.

It was not enough to be able to eavesdrop and decipher secret messages. It was also important that the authorities could detect which buildings, in which streets, they were emanating from. Hostile agents would naturally keep their activities as invisible as possible, but advances in direction-finding technology meant that it was gradually becoming more difficult to hide. Of course, in this world of scientific cloak and dagger, there were mistakes and setbacks. One ostensible triumph was when messages tracked to the All Russian Co-operative Society, near Moorgate, led to a raid, but the Soviets had carefully removed all transmission equipment before the raiders arrived. More, some of the decoded Soviet messages were read out in Parliament as evidence of perfidy (and British codebreaking genius). All that did was tell the Russians that they had to make their codes much harder to crack. They immediately did so.

When the Government Code and Cypher School codebreakers were preparing in earnest for war to come once more – rather in advance of many other institutions – the Denmark Hill Intercept Station was cloaked in a further layer of secrecy. Now, as well as answering to Scotland Yard, it would be reporting to the Foreign Office. And Commander Kenworthy would go on to establish other out-stations for the gathering of untold thousands of communications from the airwaves to be sent on to the brains' trust at Bletchley Park. His inventiveness with electrics was useful in other ways. It was at Denmark Hill that he formulated 'The J Machine' in 1935. This was a device designed to help with one of the most formidable and intractable challenges facing British codebreakers, getting a crowbar into the ciphers sent by the Japanese.

Indeed, so intense was Commander Kenworthy's passion for the electrical technology of surveillance that after the end of the Second World War, when Bletchley Park regenerated into GCHQ (Government Communications Headquarters), he carried on working for them, still very much under the Official Secrets Act, until 1957.

This outpost of secrets in the midst of the leafiest of suburbs did not outlive the war and the substantial premises were put to work in a range of different ways. But Grove Park, Denmark Hill is worth visiting now as a relatively little-known part of the greater Bletchley Park story. A short climb up the hill from the railway station gives a glimpse of the city below. The wireless geniuses who worked under Commander Kenworthy would have all gazed at that view throughout the Nazi Blitz of 1940–41, emerging from shelters and reporting for duty on mornings where the smoke from countless fires and from all those burning city buildings and churches hung in the air. For so many wireless interceptors, the war was a means of putting their great, all-abiding passions to work for the nation, but it was from these heights on Denmark Hill that they will have also seen precisely what was at stake with every single day of the conflict.

How to get there

Although the intercept station has long been transformed into private housing, Grove Park and the surrounding area are nonetheless worth a visit, first to get a sense of the interceptors and their hilltop eyrie and second to enjoy some of the marvellous eighteenth-century architecture that stretches the length of Camberwell Grove. This being south London, rail is rather more efficient than road, and the nearest station is Denmark Hill, which is served both by Southern Rail and also the London Overground network.

Learning Japanese in Bedford

The Inter-Services Special Intelligence School, Bedford, 2 Broadway

Many small market towns were required to keep secrets throughout the war but there was no one in Bedford who could have even begun to guess *why* the operations in the centre of their town were classified. The work being carried out here was so lateral and esoteric that any passing spy would have had to have been a genius to sniff it out. The site was a set of upstairs rooms above a showroom of gas cookers at the corner of the Broadway crossroads and the only incongruous element that might have made any passers-by raise their eyebrows was the military man who favoured his regiment's brightly coloured tartan dress trousers as everyday wear. This figure was not standing guard: rather he was the presiding genius of this secret outpost. He was a brigadier, and perhaps, paradoxically, he had little patience for fuss over other peoples' uniforms. Younger associates were asked why they insisted on wearing their army boots – then, getting the message, they began to wear more comfortable plimsolls instead. And not far from the statue of John Bunyan, overlooking the centre of this bustling town, a great number of young men, some in proper uniform, others with the appearance of civil servants, trooped up those stairs to where a miracle was unfolding.

For what Brigadier Tiltman was achieving up there was a feat considered impossible in many circles. He and his associates were teaching these young men useable Japanese in the space of six months (most Japanese scholars believed such an education would take three years). And the reason for the speed? This was another hugely important thread in the codebreaking network. Brigadier Tiltman was facing one of the most extraordinarily daunting challenges of the war: to break into and unravel the Japanese naval codes. What was more remarkable was that he had no academic training in linguistics. Instead, somehow, he had taught himself Japanese and about a dozen other languages.

The young men sitting above that gas-cooker showroom engaged in their intensive studies were not just Bletchley types, but also strong intellects drafted into other departments like the diplomatic service and the Foreign Office. All were receiving the incredibly secret know-how of mastering enough Japanese to turn their own hands to the Japanese cipher system. It is doubtful that in wartime Bedford, any of the townsfolk had even come across a Japanese person outside of the Hollywood films that showed in the town's picture palaces.

As one of the most senior cryptographers in the Bletchley Park operation, Brigadier Tiltman was renowned for his tutoring skills, and for his kindly patience with his sometimes daunted students. He was asking them to pull off an extraordinarily complex feat. Codebreaking was quite enough of a challenge in the Roman alphabet let alone a completely different language, but he had the knack for amused encouragement that spurred all of his colleagues on. His was one of the most remarkable – and unsung – minds of the century.

How did this operation end up in Bedford? Partly it was a question of geography because Bletchley Park lay just fifteen miles to the west. It was easily and speedily reached from London, Oxford and Cambridge by train, and it had the virtue of being both pretty and also very ordinary.

One of the key features of Brigadier John Tiltman's brilliant and long career in codebreaking (he started just after the First World War and carried on well after the Second) was his apparent inability to shirk a challenge. This was a trait formed when he was out in Siberia in 1919 helping the White Russians against the new era of Bolshevist rule. The temperatures of minus sixty aggravated his war injuries – but he also almost casually began picking up the Russian language, becoming amazingly proficient within a very short time. He was drafted into the Government Code and Cipher School and eventually he was sent out to India, where Russian manoeuvrings in the north-west required his skill in unknotting their coded messages. Not content with acquiring languages, Tiltman also had the most uncanny knack for seeing into the hearts of ciphers, detecting different rhythms and unravelling them by hand.

He always insisted he was not a mathematician, though he had done so well as an all-rounder at school that he had been offered a place at Oxford University aged just thirteen years old – unfortunately, a family bereavement and lack of money put paid to that. He also insisted that he was not a linguist, and that he found it hard to acquire languages. Yet pick them up he did, and while in India he started absorbing Chinese, enough certainly to set to work on Chinese cipher systems. This was a matter of trial and error. He set himself the task of decoding a Chinese document and spent a great deal of time worrying at it, only to be told later by a more experienced colleague who passed his desk that it was in fact a perfectly straightforward Chinese telegram instruction manual.

Yet Tiltman absorbed a terrific lesson from this: never agonise over setbacks, and never shake the belief that a problem can be overcome. And even though he juggled a great many roles at Bletchley Park, his eager students at Bedford relished the times they saw him.

One such was a callow Oxford undergraduate (not long after the war he would gain his doctorate) called Michael Loewe, who had been studying Latin and Greek, and was pulled fast into the war because he had been identified as someone who might be able to learn Japanese at speed. The whole thing, even after initial recruitment, was super-secret. He had at first been put off because he saw the person sitting next to him 'writing in Chinese characters'

LEARNING JAPANESE IN BEDFORD

Brains trust: Tiltman (right) alongside Harry Hinsley (left) and GCHQ Director Sir Edward Travis (centre), Washington, USA, November 1945. The three were in the USA negotiating the framework of the revolutionary COMINT bilateral agreement with the USA.

and instantly presumed he was there as a mistake. Young Loewe had until that point been training to be an officer in the Artillery, but he and nineteen others ended up finding themselves in what looked like a schoolroom. The teacher was a retired naval officer called Oswald Tuck, who had had some forty years' experience with the Japanese language. Obviously, there were limits to what could be imparted in six months, but for the purposes of war, certain words and terms would come up more frequently than others. 'We had no idea of the purpose of our work,' Loewe said. But the room was filled with 'Japanese dictionaries, grammar books and writings which, of course, were not easy to get hold of.' Tuck also employed carefully inscribed flash-cards with Japanese characters and translations. The students were played records of the Japanese language. It was noted elsewhere that after just five weeks, 'some were carried out screaming'.[16] But for the others, a process of osmosis had begun, and the language began to seep in. Loewe remembered that his 'classmates' later became famous after the war. There was 'Jonathan Clark, who became a Fellow of the British Academy' and 'Wilfred Noyce, one of the Everest mountaineers.'

At the end of the fast course the real work began as the young men had to use this language, still very new to them, in exercises in problem-solving and cryptology. It was at that point that the young recruits at last understood why it was that they were there. In terms of confidentiality, they were allowed to tell their families that they had picked up some Japanese, but nothing more beyond that. And so the postings began, to the far and the middle east. Loewe himself was selected to stay behind for duties at Bletchley Park, though his own wartime years were every bit as intense as those of his comrades.

Naturally, few traces remain today of the top-secret Japanese school, although the building in which it all took place is still there. Ardour House, which now hosts a jeweller rather than a gas-cooker showroom, does attract pilgrims. There are those who have visited Bletchley Park who enjoy the sense of completeness that comes with seeing this wonderfully incongruous site as well. After all, here was the crucible in which the secret war was being fought and the Japanese, like the Nazis, did not think it would be possible for anyone to penetrate their hyper-encrypted messages.

How to get there

Despite having lost some of those wartime rail links (that Oxford to Cambridge line is mooted for a regeneration), it is at least still handsomely served via Thameslink, meaning it is possible to travel there directly from Brighton via Gatwick and London with very frequent trains. The site itself is a few minutes' walk from the railway station. An added advantage of rail is that there is still a branch link to Bletchley station which – as we will see later – deserves a place of its own in the history books.

SECRET STATELY HOMES

The Duke and the Spooks

Blenheim Palace, Woodstock

There was a time when the secret service could boast handsome numbers of snobs and social climbers for whom this posting would have been a dream. Rich eighteenth-century grandeur, vast landscaped grounds, galleries and great halls and drawing rooms that one could move through with almost perfect freedom was the draw here, especially if one imagined that one was born to such splendour. The location was also in a curious way rather inspirational. This extraordinary historic estate had a spirit about it that seemed to proclaim the finest virtues of the realm. In addition to all of this, it was an infinite improvement on the previous makeshift home for the agents of MI5 where they had been forced to share prison cells with the Radio Security Service codebreaking nerds at Wormwood Scrubs. Early on in the war the agents, and all the crucial secret files that they had amassed in the thirty-odd years that the agency had been in business, were evacuated to Oxfordshire. Where perhaps could have been more pleasing than the birth-place of Winston Churchill?

In a way, it was also a double-bluff of some bravura. There are few houses in the entire country less discreet or tucked away than the magnificent edifice of Blenheim Palace. This baroque creation, which was the work of John Vanbrugh and Nicholas Hawksmoor, represented the dawn of a new aesthetic sensibility and the start of the Romantic movement. It was built between 1705 and 1722, and it was a gift to the Duke of Marlborough, who had recently triumphed over French and Bavarian troops. The parklands surrounding the house were also imbued with that rich artistic sensibility. These grounds and gardens and lakes were the work of 'Capability' Brown and they were so intensely influential that Peter the Great wanted to import the style to Russia. By 1940, the house still remained the home of the Marlborough family and it represented a form of sanctuary. While London and the City, in all of the jumbled chaos of its beautiful churches, houses and factories, was being targeted with ever-increasing ferocity by the Luftwaffe, country estates like Blenheim were untouched.

Nevertheless, the decision to move MI5 there posed possible risks to this beautiful work of architecture. Should there ever have been any hint that the secret services were now operating from there – back in 1940 the existence of the agency was never even publicly referred to – the estate might have made a tempting target for any German planes returning from intensive bombing missions over Birmingham or Coventry. In addition, there were elements of security that might have been a little more difficult to control amid all the sprawling lavish splendour.

In truth, there was little splendour to be found in the makeshift wooden huts that were erected a little distance away from the main bulk of the house, and in which the administrative work of the agency would be carried out. Nor were the staff fortunate enough to be billeted in any of the grand sleeping chambers (unlike the Wrens of Woburn Abbey, as we shall see later). Female members of staff were instead allocated quarters at Keble College, Oxford, which was a few miles down the road from Woodstock. Each day, a bus would take them from Oxford city centre to the main estate gate at Blenheim (itself just a short walk down a beautiful, honeyed Cotswold-stone Woodstock street). There would be a security check here, and then after being taken by estate transport up the drive to the Palace, there would be a double-check before they got to their offices.

Those huts were within the main gates of the Palace's immediate forecourt. At various points over the first few months of the war, the grounds were shared with evacuated pupils and teachers from Repton public school, who were soon moved off to alternative accommodation. But the staff of MI5 were hermetically separated from all other Blenheim residents, up to and including the Duke of Marlborough. He must have been intrigued by the requisitioning of part of the Palace's upper floor by the secret service. It was set up as a communications centre and as an area where translators could work on messages and intercepts from overseas. Meanwhile, downstairs, the Great Hall was converted into the world's grandest filing room; it was filled with filing cabinets, the contents of which were naturally hyper-secret. Incidentally, the term 'Great Hall' hardly does justice to the scale of this space. It ascends to the full height of the palace, a dizzying vision of columns, arches, vast windows admitting dazzling light, ceiling frescos, portraits and marbled floor. The metallic clang of shutting filing cabinets echoed incongruously but prettily around it. Nearby, the Long Library was transformed into the poshest typing pool on earth. The length of this room was not exaggerated: it was some 150 feet in all. Punctuated with fireplaces on one side of the wall, and graced with vast windows along the other, the typists who worked here also had sumptuous architecture and the sight of uncountable numbers of books in great shelves for their eyes to rest on when they were glancing up from their machines.

There was a small outbreak of tension between the Duke and his spook guests when it came to a particular patch of the garden that lay close to the huts. This little area of earth, it was said among MI5 employees, was infused with soil from the site of the original battle of Blenheim. It was, in a sense, sacred ground and as such was to be largely avoided. The workmen bringing in the storage cupboards for the huts alas saw the mystic patch as a short-cut and trampled their way across it as they performed their heavy-lifting duties.

But there were others who had the keenest appreciation of the treasures of Blenheim Palace and among them was a recent recruit who happened to be an art historian. His name was Anthony Blunt. He was a double agent, having been recruited by the Soviets in the 1930s. His treachery lay exquisitely well-hidden and it was not until 1979 that he was finally unmasked as 'the Fourth Man' in the Cambridge Spy Ring. So, in one sense, all the elaborate security about the move of MI5 to Oxfordshire was rendered absurd by his very presence.

Nonetheless, as Blunt went about his daily duties, he also had the chance to drink in some of the greatest art treasures to be found in the realm, lining the walls of the Palace's galleries. Nor was he selfish about his delight, because during break time, he would take colleagues from the huts upon impromptu guided tours, explaining the techniques and the histories of the Old Masters. Although his loyalties to Moscow and the Kremlin were – over so many years – hideously damaging, Blunt's love for art was entirely, piercingly authentic. After the war, he was made Keeper of the Queen's Pictures, the traitor moving smoothly through the Royal Palaces and having many conversations with Her Majesty herself about the beauty and the provenance of her own extraordinary art collection.

For the younger administrative staff of MI5, the sojourn at Blenheim Palace also gave them access to the beautiful parklands, not merely for soulful walks during breaks, but also for messing around in the lakes. Come the winter, Capability Brown's exquisitely arranged landscape was bright white beneath skies of iron and to some of the MI5 team, this meant snowballs and, even in the harder frosts, ice-skating. Yet none of them ever forgot why they were there. And they all understood very well the paramount need for total secrecy. Not everyone was staying at Keble College. There were also recruits billeted in private houses in Oxford and Woodstock, who knew that they had to resist the natural curiosity of their landlords about the exact nature of the work that they were doing.

All of which puts an apocryphal tale about the spies and Blenheim into a fresh context. Years later, it was suggested that the bus driver who took the workers from Oxford to Woodstock each day would – upon reaching the gates of Blenheim – jokingly shout at the top of his voice: 'Alight here for MI5 HQ!' This was extremely unlikely; the war was too serious for that sort of joke. But after the war, the story was transposed and in the 1950s, the conductors on the red London buses that drove close to the new spook offices would cry: 'Alight here for Park Lane, Curzon Street and MI5!' By then, no harm could be done.

The man most agog at the spies in Blenheim Palace was the Palace's most famous baby, Winston Churchill (he was born there in 1874). Years later, it was remembered by some who worked there that whenever the agency had had a notable success in an operation, or when it was felt that the administrative staff had done a particularly good job, Churchill sent consignments of chocolate and cigars. These were commodities as luxurious as gold dust in the pinched days of rationing. The pleasure of eating and smoking gifts from a grateful Prime Minister in the grounds of that architectural magnificence must have been intensely satisfying.

As a postscript, it might be pointed out that the spies were not the only distinguished wartime secret that the Duke and his Blenheim staff kept. In 1944, those Capability Brown lakes were used for practical rehearsals for prototype landing craft that were intended for use in the forthcoming D-Day landings. There are wonderful photographs of a mighty machine emerging from the waters, and of the delighted Duke and his team clambering around on top of it, examining this engineering marvel.

HOW TO GET THERE

Naturally, as a UNESCO World Heritage Site, Blenheim Palace and its grounds are one of the most popular tourist attractions on the continent. In fact, to make a day of it, it is also worth checking out some of the wonderful gastropubs and restaurants in the town of Woodstock, immediately next to the estate. The estate lies eight miles north-west of Oxford on the A44 Evesham Road. The nearest railway station is Oxford Parkway, some five miles away.

The Dances and the Deer

Woburn Abbey, Buckinghamshire

It is easy to forget now just how young many of the people drawn into the secret side of the Second World War were. Huge numbers of them were teenagers pulled away from the familiarity of home, thrown into new surroundings with platoons of strangers and told that they had to keep their work top secret, under pain of unnamed punishments. On top of this, there was an element sometimes of entering some fantasy world. Imagine being brought up in a small industrial town, the air thick with smog, and then finding oneself living in a centuries-old stately home, set in its own supremely silent parkland, the air crystalline and the countryside rich and inviting. This particular classical pile was Woburn Abbey, in the north of Buckinghamshire. The young women brought to live here had signed up for the Wrens and had passed a very particular aptitude test (as we have seen, any keenness for cryptic crosswords was pounced upon by the authorities). The work they were going to be set was gruelling in the extreme, but Woburn Abbey and its surrounds would provide the escape, not merely through the exhilarating beauty of the house, but also through the romances that would be found in its near vicinity.

Like all requisitioned country houses in the war, Woburn Abbey was expected to play host to a range of people and activities. But as the war went on, and as the codebreaking operation at nearby Bletchley Park expanded into an industrial-scale proposition, hundreds of young Wrens were needed for a multiplicity of tasks, not just tending to vast Bombe machines, but also working on transcribing Japanese codes. All this work was carried out on a twenty-four-hour cycle, split up into three shifts of eight hours. Those coming off the notoriously draining night shifts would be returned to Woburn Abbey by 8 a.m., get some breakfast, and then flop exhausted into their beds. Hanging over all this was the intense secrecy, so much so that Wrens working in different sections were not allowed under any circumstances to discuss that work. And obviously, their families back home had not the slightest notion.

For anyone aged eighteen or nineteen, all of this might have seemed quite a formidable proposition and the pressure was tightened by knowing that any tiny mistakes in even the most routine clerical cryptographical job might have horrible unforeseen consequences out in the field. So, it was as well that the Abbey itself was seen as a congenial and warm space, far from the relentless tension of work.

The Abbey had once been a monastery. Abolished in Henry's dissolution, the house that then stood on the site was handed by Henry's young son Edward to the Russell family. The house became a palimpsest, constantly being rebuilt, but always around the old structure. The 1620s version was, in part, incorporated into the mid-eighteenth-century reconstruction, led by architects Henry Holland and Henry Flitcroft. The house had regenerated into the grand Palladian style – all stucco and doric columns, forming a glorious square, and looking out over fecund fields and woods. Further alterations came in the nineteenth century and the interior was similarly sumptuous, if perhaps a shade chintzy when compared to the even grander Blenheim Palace.

And it was in this house that young Wrens found themselves deposited, without having had any clue where it was that they were being taken. One recalled that her bus had arrived up the Abbey's driveway late one night and so the first sight she had of her new home for the foreseeable future was of this extraordinary edifice, pale and vast under soft moonlight. She recalled that while it was grand on the outside, the interior was a different matter. This was several years into the war, and vast numbers of personnel marching through with a hundred different practical requirements had denuded it of the most immediately obvious luxuries. But there were still imposing portraits and state rooms (nominally forbidden for Wrens to lounge around in) and there was one bathroom that was about the size of the houses that some of the young Wrens had originally come from. That bathroom elicited both delight and also intense self-consciousness. But all strange things become familiar in the end. Nor were the Wrens allowed to sleep in the statelier bedrooms. Instead, they were stationed in the attic rooms with four sets of bunks and eight young ladies to each room. One slight advantage was that the heat of the house below during the day tended to rise, so the attics were not too chilly at night.

There was also, for some, an agreeable boarding-school atmosphere about the place. Many of the Wrens had only just left their own (non-boarding) schools, but here there was a sense of intense bonding, especially given the rigour of the work and the need for relaxation afterwards. Even if the young women were just sitting quietly knitting or reading a book, making an attempt to decompress after eight hours in hot machine rooms tending to temperamental technology, there was a shared sense that they were all in it together on a great enterprise.

Margaret O'Connell was one such recruit and for her, Woburn Abbey seemed more like a ship because, of course, it was officially part of the Royal Navy. 'The rooms were referred to as cabins and when we went out the front door, we were said to have gone ashore,' she recalled. There was discipline and regimentation – strictness about Sunday-morning church attendance seemed not especially popular, particularly among those who had only just come off their shifts at Bletchley Park – but to counter that, 'there was a terrific feeling of friendship and unity'.[17]

Added to this, the house had its own little outbreaks of eccentricity. Wren Jean Shakespeare was one of the few who managed to get a place in a bunk in a room rather grander than the attic. 'We stayed in the Duke's dressing room,' she said, 'and I remember it was done out in Victorian parrot wallpaper.' The opulence of the bathroom and any chance to luxuriate, however, was rather marred by wartime restrictions. The women were only allowed five inches of water in the bathtub. On top of that, in the winters, the high-ceilinged rooms were rather difficult to heat. Some remembered the terrible contrast between the stifling temperatures of the Bletchley machine rooms and the raw chilliness of many parts of Woburn Abbey.

There was frequently romance in the air. Dances were held at Woburn Abbey, which attracted not only young codebreakers like Peter Hilton, but officers from all around, including Americans. There were other encounters too. Wren Margaret Douglas, who had sailed from Argentina to join the war effort, and who was now posted at Woburn, met an officer of the Royal Canadian Air Force in the pitch darkness of the blacked-out railway station at Bletchley. The officer was waiting for a London-bound train and the two struck up an enthusiastic conversation. The train arrived before they exchanged names. But he could not get her out of his head and so, later, he wrote a letter addressed to 'The blonde Wren from Argentina on the platform at Bletchley Station' which somehow, incredibly, made its way to her at Woburn Abbey. The fire of love was lit and just before the war ended in 1945, Margaret Douglas married Craig Cooper, her hitherto unnamed suitor.

Later in the war there were dances in nearby Bedford as well. These hops featured large numbers of American servicemen billeted nearby and were regarded as a fantastic treat after onerous weeks at Woburn and the Park. One venue featured a number of paper cut-out hearts dangling from the ceiling. Another specialised in exotic refreshments that British Wrens had never come across before including sweet maple syrup and milkshakes in a variety of flavours. But the core of these evenings was formed by the addictive sound of Swing and big band music. Throughout the war, the British had developed a kind of dance mania and this imported style could not be resisted by the young. There were some at Woburn Abbey who were thrilled beyond words when they discovered that there would be a concert near Bedford for American servicemen and guests given by none other than the great Glenn Miller.

Meanwhile, the stables of the Woburn Abbey estate offered their own opportunities for healthy and innocent escapism. Some of the Wrens were there long enough to acquire ponies and others learned how to ride and revelled in the free time they got to go galloping off into the gentle green countryside. There were others who developed a taste for hunting and the local area was not short of Hunts to join.

None of this was frivolous as these hundreds of young women across the years of the war needed all the outlets for relaxation and fun that they could get, for the work that they were carrying out around the clock was both physically debilitating and an assault on their mental health. Rather than having the giddy intellectual excitement of cracking the codes themselves, they were ensuring that the process of industrial code-cracking was kept running smoothly, and this in itself could be thankless. It meant working in a constant haze of sprayed machine oil and through the night with proto-computers that could break down multiple times for no apparent reason just as there seemed to be the greatest urgency to get the codes processed, be they messages from U-boats or from deep within Europe. This was a production line where any slip or outbreak of cack-handedness might cost lives, so these young women held quite a weight on their shoulders.

Thus, even the more startling aspects of life at Woburn Abbey, like being woken by the sound and sight of rutting deer in the park, for instance, were quite welcome, and the camaraderie meant that the pressure to keep their working lives top secret was made just that little bit easier.

HOW TO GET THERE

Woburn Abbey as an attraction has been shut for some time for vital renovations to be carried out. But it will be open to the public again in 2022 with many new features as well as exciting restorations. Part of the appeal – as well as simple enjoyment of the Humphrey Repton-designed landscape around the house

– will be imagining what it was like to suddenly find oneself posted there. By car, Woburn Abbey lies four miles west of the M1 and is between junctions 12 and 13. The nearest railway station is Flitwick, although there are also regular services connecting across the country from Bletchley seven miles away.

Intelligence from the Heavens

Danesfield House, Medmenham, near Marlow,
Buckinghamshire

Much of the secret war was about unravelling the mysteries of messages within messages or faraway voices transmitting codes on atmospheric airwaves. But there were puzzles in images too, and at a particularly large and florid gothic nineteenth-century house close to the slow, silent waters of the rural Thames, there was a brilliant team of men and women who were gazing deep into the heart of the Nazi war machine without leaving their desks. Like all clandestine work, it was vital that no suggestion of what they were doing should ever leak out. The Germans had already proved adept and cunning at camouflaging their own classified projects. But at RAF Medmenham, the team was also providing the most incredible real-time visual record of the unfolding conflict. The images they pored over have now become extraordinary historical records. What made the establishment even more noteworthy was not just the fact that it employed the Prime Minister's daughter, but also that in some of its most crucial exercises, women led the way.

Photo sensitive: Danesfield House became a secret film development factory.

The grey-stoned edifice of Danesfield House – a 1901 blend of Tudor and Renaissance stylings built for a soap magnate – lies close to the exquisite riverine town of Marlow and is not very many miles upstream from the equally lovely Henley-upon-Thames. This part of the country was (and is) an idyll of trailing willows and little wooded islands and of rowing boats and picnics in meadows. In the straitened years of war, this lush, wooded valley, and the cheerfully preposterous house that overlooked it, might have seemed to some to represent a sort of English paradise. When the war broke out, it had originally been requisitioned for a London boys' school.

But they were all very soon moved out to make way for a specialised branch of the RAF: the Photo Intelligence and Interpretation Unit. As well as RAF staff members, the team was joined by some academics from the field of geology.

The task in a broad sense was that of airborne espionage. British aeroplanes flying over enemy territory would be fitted with underside cameras which would photograph the terrain thousands of feet below. Ingeniously, they would frequently use stereoscopic cameras. This meant that when they returned to base, and when the camera images were developed, those viewing them could see in 3D through the special lenses that gave an illusion of depth. Whereas flat images of landscapes could give little indication of unexplained humps in the ground that could hint at concealed weapons facilities or even underground factories, the 3D photographs would give interpreters a much clearer understanding of the territory. It was also useful in terms of then sending out instructions to undercover operatives in the field, or even units preparing to attack. More than this, this intelligence could also pick up even the most carefully camouflaged movements of troops and heavy weaponry. Before the days of ubiquitous CCTV, or drones, this was the means by which the British sought to keep the Nazis permanently within sight.

The big house with surrounding huts was a forward echo of what a couple of post-war British film studios would look like and was to become a quite extraordinary factory of imagery. The department arrived at Danesfield

House in April 1941, after being evacuated from the rather less pretty London suburb of Wembley. It was known as the Central Interpretation Unit. To begin with, there were some forty photographic interpreters. Danesfield House was pleasing not just because of the wood-panelled grandeur of its interior, but also because of the light-filled rooms on the second floor with large, mullioned windows overlooking meadows and the river and the wide skies above. The natural light was a great advantage when peering into those stereoscopic viewers.

The operation was under the control of Wing Commander Douglas Kendall. Even before the move out to this secluded location, his unit had had notable successes. Images taken from planes above France in the late summer of 1940 had been focusing on movement towards the coast. Were the Nazis building up an invasion force in the aftermath of the humiliating British retreat from Dunkirk? The photographic evidence suggested this was so, but it also captured, day by day, the gradual dispersal of the troops and the ordnance as the autumn swirled in, indicating that whatever attack there may have been across the Channel had now been called off. This, naturally, was a crucial line of intelligence being relayed to Downing Street and it had come through some terrific feats of bravery. Spitfire pilots flew out with the guns removed from their planes to make room for the cameras. They were assured that they had no need of guns while they were zooming at such speeds through the sky. This was not strictly true, and the heroism involved in making repeated sorties over occupied territory perhaps – owing to the secrecy – never quite received its full due. By the time that the photographic team had moved to Danes-field, their modest operation was expanding at a vast rate, matching the numbers of theatres of war around the globe.

One of the most distinguished figures at RAF Medmen-ham (as the house was designated) was a former journalist from a magazine called *The Aeroplane* and unusually for the time, that journalist was a woman. Her name was Constance Babington Smith. She was a Flight Officer, having volunteered for the WAAFs in order to utilise both her expertise and tremendous enthusiasm. And as the war went on, she was responsible for some of the unit's most brilliant successes.

In 1943, for instance, she was analysing photographs taken of the Peenmunde airfield in northern Germany, and she was quick to spot an anomaly of scorch marks burnt into the runway grass. This surely could only mean a leap in technology that she perhaps had daydreamed about herself: the successful development of the jet engine. Churchill's rather singular scientific adviser, Lord Cherwell – whose rudeness and contempt alienated many – was particularly sniffy about this amazing discovery. He refused to believe it and suggested that Constance Babington Smith had fallen for a simple hoax. Possibly he could not imagine that a woman could make such a deduction. But he was very wrong and she was very right. The Nazis had painstakingly fashioned a twin-engine jet plane. And in the latter stages of the war, it was the fastest plane in the sky, with speeds of around 600 miles per hour.

There were more ominous clues to more terrible weapons at Peenmunde just months later, which again Constance Babington Smith was able to decipher from aerial stereoscopic imagery. This time it was not scorch marks but launch infrastructure. She could also detect in the images the suggestion of a vast missile. Again, she was fast with her conclusions and reported to her superiors that the Nazis had managed to invent a flying bomb. This was the first inkling of the V-1 weapon that would soon be whistling through the stratosphere and descending fast upon London. And these in turn would be followed by the V-2 missiles, delivering death by remote control for

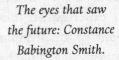
The eyes that saw the future: Constance Babington Smith.

the first time. Babington Smith's initial alert led to the fast creation of a new team at Danesfield House, called Crossbow, and its mission was to monitor and study the V-weapons programme in order to find weaknesses and vulnerabilities. The Nazis had spread the V-weapons and their launch ramps over many sites and Constance Babington Smith and her team raced to pinpoint them all.

Perhaps naturally, such a charismatic presence at Danesfield House was subject to much attention and one frequent visitor was the inventor of the British version of the jet engine, Frank Whittle. In many ways, Babington Smith represented his absolute ideal of womanhood. He described her thus: 'An attractive young lady who combined considerable personal charm with an intense interest in aircraft.'[18] It was also said that of the many questions he asked when around her, most frequent was the name of the scent that she used. Perhaps this came under Babington Smith's personal Secrets Act. But she eventually revealed elsewhere that the perfume in question was L'Heure Bleu by Guerlain. What she wanted, she said, was to offset the rather masculine RAF uniform with a perfectly feminine scent. Her expertise led to an MBE, and she even later did some work for the American government. The secret work at Danesfield House had shown the authorities the great depth of her capability.

Nor was she alone. Another brilliant woman at Danesfield House was Professor Dorothy Garrod, a pioneering archaeologist at a time when few women were encouraged into the discipline. The archaeology gave her a particularly sharp eye for landscapes and the shifts and anomalies that might disclose either ancient or very recent history. The job before her had the potential to be especially vexing, with countless images of the desert sands of north Africa requiring analysis. But she had had an extraordinary range of experience that made her perfect for the job. In the 1930s, she had led an expedition into the wilderness of Mount Carmel in British mandate Palestine (now Israel). The prehistoric skulls that she and her team excavated enabled them to deduce not only how this particular local tribe had worked and hunted, but also what they ate, and something of their social relations. Professor Garrod had reached deep through the darkness of time to clasp hands with the far-distant dead. To do so required a serious gift for lateral thinking and visualisation, and she would use that gift again in Kurdistan among other regions. But it was this talent that she also brought to bear on the war.

The objective was to try to track the movements of Rommel's forces as precisely as possible. Given the possibilities for concealment and given the way that shifting sands might erase traces of any human presence, Professor Garrod had to not only be keen-eyed but also brilliantly analytical when it came to the evidence of topography and how it may help or hinder military movements. When the conflict was over, she returned to the trenches and the pits of the past.

There was another woman, young and deeply diligent, who attracted curious attention. This was Sarah Oliver, who had earned promotion to Photographic Interpreter without any suggestion of family connections. Given that her father was Winston Churchill, this was quite an achievement. Those who worked with her remembered that she would never have considered pulling rank in any way. More than that, she worked with some intensity, as well as enthusiasm. Optimism in any kind of secret interpretation work is beyond value as it suggests that even the most daunting challenges can eventually be overcome.

The Photographic Unit was also monitoring the darker side of the Allied war that included the vast raids mounted by Bomber Command upon cities right the way across Germany, from 1942 right until the very end of the war. The terrifying firestorm raised in the old timber-built city of Hamburg in 1942 began to convince some in Bomber Command and in Whitehall that the path to a swifter victory and Nazi capitulation lay in what was termed 'morale bombing'. This meant targeting not only military sites and vast factories but also residential housing and residential districts, and all the civilians therein. The idea of the photography to begin with was to give a general indication of how effective any bombing raid had been. Had the targeted factories or power stations been hit or missed? The photography was pitilessly accurate, unlike the pre-computer planes of Bomber Command. But there was another dimension too. The photos taken in subsequent raids – especially those showing the inferno started in Dresden in February 1945 – went on to inform wider views about the waging of total war. These frightful images of ash and fire, lightning explosive flashes in the darkness of night, told the public that this was not a gentlemanly war, rather the enemy had to be stamped out no matter what.

And it is for that reason that the images live on now, for they formed an instant and unflinching historical record. Stereoscopic viewers were not required in these instances for interpretation. These pictures taken from the air, of shattered stone under weirdly twilit skies, told the whole story.

But Danesfield House and its gardens swooping down to turbid waters were a balm. Even if by the end of the war, the house was almost surrounded by a maze of multiple huts and a production line of developing film, there was fun to be had too. The house lay quite close to the site of the notorious eighteenth-century Hellfire Club – which in its day had featured debauches involving daft pagan sex rituals and much drink – and by means of tribute, the interpreters formed their own version of this society using the Great Hall of Danesfield House for their (very mild, non-pagan, non-sexy and strictly rationed) debauches. Somehow, given the height involved, someone managed to leave their footprint on the ceiling.

Added to this, several officers were able to live in the house, with rooms available in the clock tower. It is said that of all the places to be billeted throughout the war, this must have been one of the most supremely desirable, with baronial surrounds and views that the Thames painter Stanley Spencer would have fainted for.

These days, the house is a very swanky hotel (which, ahem, I have had the privilege of staying in, while engaged upon a newspaper assignment many years ago). But the past is still honoured there, indeed there is much reason to take pleasure in the story of the eyes in the skies above.

How to get there

If perhaps you are not tempted to stay the night at Danesfield House, an afternoon tea might be equally enjoyable. The hotel lies on the A4155 Henley Road, a little outside of Marlow-upon-Thames. The traffic in the area can frequently be snarled. The nearest railway station is in the town of Marlow itself and is a charming little branch line trailing out from Maidenhead, and just a couple of miles or so away from Danesfield House.

The Ears of the Army

Beaumanor Hall, Leicestershire

The atmosphere, for such a carefully guarded military establishment, could very occasionally be raucous, and the young men and women posted here were perhaps more direct with one another in terms of humour than at more rarefied sites. Even more unusually for a gravely serious secret institution, there was a satirical staff magazine packed with jokes and scandal. This was Beaumanor Hall, a place that was, in operational terms, a cousin to Bletchley Park. Whereas Bletchley seemed a celebration of all that was brilliantly eccentric, the young people whose jobs were to tune in to the enemy's army radio signals at Beaumanor Hall had quite a different sort of energy as they were eager for escapism in any form. This was understandable, for even in an age before there was understanding of repetitive strain injury, their confidential work could often be utterly and lethally repetitive and boring. It was the prospect of spare time high-jinks – whether composing limericks for the house journal or getting ready for the local Loughborough hop – that kept them sane. This was the boiler house of the secret war: completely vital and yet also rather thankless.

The house itself bemused some of those recruited to work within it. It was a Victorian mansion, which was rather more pleasing than the effort at Bletchley, square but ornamented. And some of those who came there were specialists in their field of capturing enemy communications. They were termed WOYGs. This was an acronym for War Office Y Group. The Y Service as we have seen earlier provided the codebreakers with their raw material. Working with them were Experimental Wireless Assistants. And working alongside all of them were great numbers of Auxiliary Territorial Service volunteers – young women from around the country, impatient to throw themselves into the war effort. Yet despite the military aspect of the work, there was from the start something winningly chaotic about this establishment humming with hundreds of radio receivers and surrounded by wooden huts disguised as cricket pavilions and garden equipment sheds.

Beaumanor Hall was noted for an unusually high incidence of discarded teacups and mislaid bureaucratic paperwork. Whenever a senior figure from London was due to pay a visit, there would be an undignified scramble as a frantic tidy-up got underway. Another official, arriving there late at night, was in hope of some refreshment, despite the hour, and he received a tomato and pilchard sandwich and a beaker of whiskey.

Yet the discipline and the secrecy were as intense as any other establishment. Here in this world of thermionic valves and chattering teleprinters, wireless assistants and ATS women were posted at radio sets in strict rows, for strict hours, tuning into designated German Army frequencies and transcribing all the Morse traffic that went through their headsets. Mistakes were simply not allowed. This was the means of gaining minute-by-minute intelligence on all the movements of the Wehrmacht. As a result, on busy shifts, with the radio waves whispering with countless communications, the work – transcribing Morse on to special notepads at a blurred speed – could be hunched and hard on certain muscles. The end of the shift, if it was in the day, required more than rest. These women and men needed furious physical activity to breathe fresh life into cramped tendons.

The soldiers billeted in the house had their own ideas. Troop trucks carrying the ATS women to and from their billets would be greeted with shrill wolf whistles, and the women would retaliate with vulgar insults shouted up at the windows. There was little in the way of on-base romances; the work patterns would never allow for that. Off-base was quite a different matter though. Most of the women and men who worked at Beaumanor were billeted in nearby small towns and villages like Woodhouse Eaves and Quorn in frequently freezing boarding houses. The answer to the boredom and the cold was dancing, and lots of it. The nearby town of Loughborough thankfully provided the halls and the loud swing music.

Rambunctious: Beaumanor Hall in Leicestershire.

But there was a huge amount of sport too. Unlike the more academic and nerdier inmates at Bletchley Park, the secret staff of Beaumanor Hall loved outdoor games. As well as football, netball, tennis and cycling, it had its own dedicated (and secret) rambling society. Few of the Beaumanor recruits – drawn from all corners of the country – had ever really seen or heard much about the country's unsung midlands but when they discovered neighbouring Charnwood Forest, and the rich green of the farmland all around, they fell for it quickly.

Some were more high-minded than others. Chris Barnes had arrived at Beaumanor having excelled in various aptitude tests to do with Morse and intelligence.

'It was intense,' he recalled. 'You sat down at a receiver with a pad in front of you and you struggled to hear the very often weak signals . . . you were normally given the frequency because you were watching specific tasks . . . The most important thing we tracked was the U-boats . . . I think we knew they were U-boats, but we didn't understand the importance of it.'[19] As well as lacking the precise detail or context – secrecy at all levels was key – Mr Barnes remembered that Bletchley Park was never mentioned, even though this was where the fruit of his work was going.

This bright young man enjoyed the demanding work, but he too very much needed his leisure hours to be a complete contrast. At first, his new surroundings were a bit of a shock, especially as he had been brought up amid the rich orchards of rural Kent, 'and I found myself dumped in Loughborough, which was not the most cheering of places.' Happily, he was billeted in the village of Woodhouse Eaves and soon he fell into the rhythm of his new life. His own form of escapism was classical music, a passion he shared with fellow Beaumanor operative Harry Dodd. Throughout his period posted there, Barnes set out to educate himself in the works of as many composers as possible. In that time, nearby Leicester could not only offer popular dances and cinema, but also high-minded concerts.

There was one abiding local difficulty: he and the other wireless experts who worked at Beaumanor were not in uniform. Naturally they were not allowed to tell anyone anything about the nature of the work that they were doing. But this meant that outside of Beaumanor, people wondered why these perfectly fit young men were not in military service. Mr Barnes's landlady was always rather cool with him. So, indeed, was the landlord of the local pub where he and his colleagues would repair for pints. That landlord's coolness turned icy when he perceived – correctly – that these intellectual-looking men were stringing out their pints for hours.

The locals were desperate for information; what was the nature of the work going on in the big house that required it to be defended at all hours by an entire platoon of the Home Guard? Who were these men and women spending sunny Sundays walking out into Charnwood Forest? The exterior of the Hall was festooned with radio aerials, which might have given some form of clue. But even these were interpreted at an angle with locals speculating that they were something to do with extraordinary secret experiments.

As a result, there were comical interludes when local workmen were summoned to attend to tasks at the Hall. The area's veteran chimney sweep was one day invited in to fix the smoky fireplaces. The old chap, who with his brushes had to be followed at every step, was prevented from entering any of the Map Rooms or Operation Rooms, and any stray bits of paperwork (of which there were many) had to be quickly removed from his suspicious gaze. The natural result of this was that local rumours multiplied. One theory was that the aerials outside

Beaumanor Hall were transmitting directly to every British secret agent, giving them their super-confidential instructions. More gothically, some postulated that Beaumanor Hall was being used as a prison for the Nazi Rudolf Hess, who had quixotically flown to Britain. The idea was that he 'was being tortured daily'. The very idea, recalled Corporal Harold Everett, made him and his colleagues laugh out loud. 'I doubt between all of us, we should even have got a toenail each.'[20]

But there were tortures of another sort at Beaumanor, in the form of some rather unkind practical jokes. On shifts when the airwaves had gone quiet – especially in the small hours – it was sometimes difficult for some to keep themselves awake. This much is only natural, as sitting in a low-lit wooden hut throughout a long night with the radio simply hissing is bound to be hypnotic and easily sleep-inducing. But sometimes more mischievous listeners would see their victim nodding off and very carefully and quietly, they would arrange the headphones and the jack of their victim so the jack was tuned not to the radio but to a nearby teleprinter. Replaced halfway in, the jack made a curious chuntering noise. The victim would wake, fiddle around and place the jack fully in and get the full blast of the teleprinter at top volume. 'He would spend the rest of the shift scraping his brain off the ceiling and walls,' noted one perpetrator coolly.[21]

Some of the ATS women had even more brutal self-inflicted methods of keeping their eyes open on those 2 a.m. shifts. Rene Pederson recalled: 'The night duty was a devil as very often we had not had much sleep before midnight and sometimes in fact had been out on the town in the evening. I think we all smoked. I burned my elbow to keep awake.'[22]

For some of the young women, Beaumanor Hall was a formative experience full of rich friendships that otherwise might never have been made. 'We used to play noughts and crosses, do crosswords, tell our life stories,' remembered Joan Nicholls. 'And we would plan our futures. Some who were particularly naïve would be told the facts of life, especially when marriage was looming.'[23] Many recalled that teenagers in the 1940s were very much more naïve about matters of sex than later generations. Some women who were less naïve remembered the various means by which the authorities sought to discourage on-base infatuations. It was felt by many in the Wrens, for instance, that the uniform regulation underwear was quite deliberately designed as a passion-killer. The vast bloomers concerned were termed 'black-outs'.

How to get there

Beaumanor Hall is now largely a conference centre, but it is unusually run by the local authority, so it also offers a range of special themed days, cream teas and outdoor activities (as well as being a wedding venue). It is just outside the village of Woodhouse Eaves, which itself is worth having a look around. As well as being architecturally charming and interesting, it also has its claim to codebreaking history since many of the

Y Service operatives were billeted there in cottages. It is just several miles south of the town of Loughborough. Rail services are regular, via Midland Mainline. By car from the M1 (junction 22), follow the A511 towards Coalville, then the B591, follow the sign to Woodhouse Eaves and continue into next-door Woodhouse – the manor house is signposted in the village. For full information on Beaumanor events and accessibility, visit www.beaumanorhall.co.uk.

The Toyshop of Death

The Firs, Whitchurch, Buckinghamshire

Fans of the James Bond films always look forward to the sequence when MI6's in-house inventor and armourer 'Q' introduces 007 to his outlandish new weapons. It is an essential component of the fantasy. And yet it was inspired by wartime reality. Straightforward guns and grenades and bombs were one thing, but there were occasions that called for more ingenious and laterally minded devices.

Winston Churchill had set the Special Operations Executive into action, but agents and other operatives engaged in subversion and sabotage needed some bespoke and sometimes baroque means of causing blasts. And so it was that in a quiet corner of the Chiltern Hills, not far from the somnolent town of Aylesbury, a team of boffins came together at a pleasant Tudorbethan house called – perfectly innocuously – The Firs. Their work went on to make the villagers jump out of their skins on a regular basis as unpredicted explosions shook the house and grounds. Curiosity from locals only intensified on the occasion when in the wake of a mad discovery involving aniseed, the boffins scoured local shops for aniseed balls, depriving the local schoolchildren of their sweets.

The key figures in charge of this apparently anarchic institution were Major General Millis Jefferis and Stuart Macrae. Macrae was a brilliant engineer and journalist who in peacetime had communicated his fervent passion for physics through editorship of a magazine called *Armchair Science*. He also had an inordinate love for caravans, which led to his recruitment of a key boffin called Cecil Clarke, who had in peacetime perfected a new type of caravan suspension. Curiously, the atmosphere of The Firs would lend even the wildest notions involving limpet mines and sticky bombs a surreal sort of domesticity. The code designation of the department was 'MD1' and had sprung forth from the Military Intelligence Research department at the start of the war.

The military men and boffins who came to The Firs wasted no time; among the first of their creations in 1940 was 'The W Bomb'. This was a new sort of mine intended for use in German rivers to disrupt their shipping routes. But very early on, the scientists under Major Macrae were contriving to make the most lethal ingenuity seem eccentrically homely, like a pipe and slippers. Because rather than this being a hard industrial operation, amply supplied with parts and machinery, the experts simply went out to local hardware stores in Aylesbury to find the equipment they needed. This could mean anything from hundreds of condoms to porridge oats to the town's supply of aluminium washing-up bowls. Cecil Clarke insisted – in a foreshadowing of the fictional secret agent Jason Bourne – that the deadliest weapons could be fashioned from everyday household objects.

A super-secret development that would be celebrated for its inventiveness in the years to come was the limpet mine. The notion was that if an agent or soldier could swim underwater to the hull of an enemy vessel, would it be possible for him to attach a bomb to the hull and have it detonated without getting killed himself? The bomb would have to stick, as the name suggested, like a limpet. Clarke brooded and came up with the suggestion of a soluble pellet in the mechanism that would act like a sort of underwater countdown. The pellet would dissolve in the sea water and once it had done so, the mechanism inside the bomb would drop to touch the detonator, giving the brave secret agent plenty of time to swim for safety.

But what could the pellet be made from? In that country-house laboratory, all sorts of substances were experimented upon but they either dissolved far too fast or simply not at all. The solution, apparently, was pure serendipity and came about because the bulbous Clarke had a penchant for boiled sweets. One day, when poised over the problem, he knocked some off his desk and they rattled on the floor. Macrae, normally more of a man for whiskey and gin, helped to pick them up but could not resist popping an aniseed ball in his mouth. It was a eureka moment, as they realised that this was a substance that would dissolve in liquid at a steady and stable rate.

Lethal ingenuity: the development of limpet mines.

Thus it was that the team set off to scour all the local sweet shops for all the gobstoppers that they could find. But there was one problem left: with the aniseed balls in the mechanism, how could they be kept dry underwater until the diver had reached his target and was ready to attach the mine? The answer necessitated another epic shopping trip; this time around the barber shops of Bedford. It was a quest to find as many condoms as possible. The result, Macrae said later, was that the team at The Firs gained a reputation in the Chilterns for being 'sexual athletes.'[24]

There was a sort of lethal Heath Robinson allure about many of the other ideas. There was a shortage of effective anti-tank weapons, for instance, and in the event of an invasion, what else might be pressed into service to cripple Nazi vehicles? The answer was a sticky bomb. This simply was a concoction of nitroglycerin decanted into a small glass globe which was then coated with an adhesive compound. Hurl the globe at the tank and it would stick to the side and moments after that, it would explode. These sticky bombs looked extra-innocuous in storage because they were fitted with knitted woollen covers, like tea cosies, to protect the adhesive mixture. Churchill so adored the idea of the sticky bomb that he commanded that a million of them should be made.

And given that The Firs lay so close to the Prime Minister's weekend country residence at Chequers, there were also opportunities for the boffins to set up demonstrations of their new firepower in the grounds. On one such afternoon, General de Gaulle was present with Churchill as the men from The Firs set a novel form of bazooka upon what looked like a rickety tripod. One scientist indicated a distant tree and asked the Prime Minister if he could have permission to aim for it. Churchill graciously consented. But in a moment of fumbling nervousness, the boffin set the fuse running before the distinguished guest had had a chance to get safely clear. There was an almighty bang, the projectile was launched from the contraption, and it whistled past the ear of the startled General. A micro-second later, and the targeted tree went up in a billowing inferno. The social awkwardness of the near accidental assassination was occluded by the sheer pyromaniac delight of all the men as the distant tree crackled with flames.

Other triumphs included U-boat targeting mortars termed 'Hedgehogs' and a new type of anti-tank launcher called 'PIAT'. There was also the brilliant innovation of the L-Delay fuse, which meant that bombs could be set to explode with dramatically lengthened countdowns. By the middle of the war, some 250 men and women were working in and around The Firs, and the property was very tightly guarded. Major General Jefferis was, like many of his staff, so wholly absorbed in his work that he sometimes completely forgot to stop, ploughing on through day and night and noticing neither. This was a realm in which white-coated operatives had pockets stuffed with wires, chemical phials, random components and cigarettes. The Major General's wife Ruth began feeling put out that the inventions at The Firs were receiving her husband's undivided attention. The only way she could think of inching back into his life was by taking a job there helping to build the gizmos, and this she did.

But there was no question that he had found his perfect calling. Major General Jefferis – as his rank suggested – had had a distinguished career entwining soldiering and inventing. Born in 1899, he was drafted into the First World War, but at its latter stages, so he saw little of the trenches. After the war, he was sent east to India, and in the wild mountainous terrain of Waziristan, he developed a talent for inventive engineering. Part of his job there was to construct bridges not only through awkward topography, but also under the added pressure of rebel gunfire. He succeeded in designing and overseeing the construction of crucial transport infrastructure even as the bullets hissed over the top of his head, and he was heavily decorated for it. As the Second World War broke out, he saw action in Norway and, in a neat reversal, his mission now was not to build bridges but to destroy them. Thus his innate fascination for physics was turned to the subject of explosives and how most effectively to deploy them. This was how he came to form the core of MD1, that was a department, incidentally, under the control of Winston Churchill himself and the chief scientific adviser Lord Cherwell rather than a wider War Office bureaucracy. Churchill's Toyshop even had its own special dedicated funding. Those boffins were adored.

As well as the thunder-cracks of unexpected detonations, and the occasional flashes that from a distance resembled the sparks generated in Frankenstein's laboratory, the locals in Whitchurch could not begin to fathom what was happening at The Firs. Late in the war, a pair of local schoolboys could not stand it any more and, as children do, they managed to find the weak spot in the fencing around the grounds. Their goal was a Nissen hut in the shadow of the big house; they decided they had to know what was going on within it. This was a late afternoon when security was less intense and the hut by chance was not occupied. Gordon Rogers, one of the boys, recalled many decades later their feeling of awe when they stepped into this store of fuses and anti-tank devices. 'We were pretty naughty,' confessed Mr Rogers – for they were not able to resist snaffling a couple of the fuses and gizmos and placing them within their schoolbags.[25] With this, the prototype secret agents managed to creep out unseen and back through the fence. Rogers told his friend to hide their amazing haul under his bed.

Days later, it was time to get the haul out and head off for a local meadow. They had also managed to purloin small explosives which – with all the sociopathic abandon that schoolboys are noted for – they insisted on setting off without any thought for life or limb. They were remarkably unscathed but, during wartime, it was hardly likely that random explosions in a field would go uninvestigated. The truth gradually seeped out and Rogers found himself in serious trouble. He was bound over to keep the peace. It was just possible that the local authorities had understood something of his glee. But even with all of this, the secrets of The Firs remained wholly and deeply classified. The wild inventions and the extraordinary laboratories could not be discussed. And with Prime Minister Winston Churchill ejected from office at the end of the war, it had no one to advocate for its continued existence into a new Cold War. Churchill's Toyshop was closed, and the sparky range of its work only started to peep out publicly in the 1970s.

The house still stands today, at the top of Whitchurch High Street. It has been through various incarnations across the years and its latest would appear to be the ubiquitous one of luxurious apartments. Happily, though, its history is worn proudly. The village of Whitchurch itself is worth walking around to feel some of the mad context of the explosive work in the big house. The village over-looks the Vale of Aylesbury and the Chiltern Hills and the skies above wheel with red kites. From the site of the early medieval motte and bailey castle to the somnolent High Street and little pub, this is in some ways the arche-type of the working English village. Not dreamily quaint, like some Cotswolds or Devon efforts, but suffused with leafy walks and a sense of its own history. The boffins fitted in a treat.

HOW TO GET THERE

Whitchurch lies on the A413 and is about four miles north of Aylesbury, which can be reached by train via a very regular service from London Marylebone station. If you want to make a day of it, do note that the nearby area also offers the attraction of Waddesdon Manor – an exquisite chateau filled with beautiful art and surrounded by mesmerising gardens on the A41. A little further north-west stands another more singular country house which deserves a full day all to itself, as we shall see presently.

An Asylum for Geniuses

Bletchley Park, Bletchley, Buckinghamshire

It is pleasingly ironic that the house which was once the most carefully kept secret in Britain is now a landmark that is recognised around the world. The mad architecture – Victorian pomposity coupled with Italian ornamentation, eaves and domes jammed together as though in a fight – now seems to underline the eccentricity of so many who worked here. Yet for the veterans who were legally required to stay silent for many decades after the war, the house also came to represent something else; a dizzy excitement and exhilaration that the drab post-war world could not match. There were some who said that the house was 'their university'. There were others who – after fifty years in the shadows – returned to it in old age with tears in their eyes, remembering every lump and bump of the driveway, every stirring of the geese on the lake, and the way that the sunlight shone on the house's curious green dome. What they had achieved here as young people helped shorten the Second World War and saved an uncountable number of lives. The work they did was peculiarly stressful, yet so many remembered the laughter. It is only really thanks to a miracle that the house is still here today, and there are countless visitors and a few surviving veterans who are profoundly grateful that it is.

The name Bletchley Park suggests grandeur, but the property itself from the start wholly lacked any pompous pretensions. Built in the late nineteenth century in the very north of Buckinghamshire, it was intended as a country bolthole for the Leon family, a place where guests could come for boisterous weekends and where in the summer locals from the small town of Bletchley could come for keenly fought cricket matches. The Leons were terrific hosts and also rather popular local employers; they kept a huge staff at the Park, including a full-time retinue of gardeners. The reason for the house's slightly eccentric architectural style was that Sir Herbert and Lady Leon were keen travellers through Europe and when they returned, they were equally keen to replicate some of the ornamental features that they had spotted.

That was the world before the Great War; the world that followed was very different. By 1937, the heir, Sir George Leon, was ready to sell. By 1938, the head of MI6 was ready to buy. Admiral Sir Hugh Sinclair was certain about the prospect that another war with Germany was inevitable and fast approaching where many hoped otherwise. The codebreaking department of intelligence, the Government Code and Cypher School, was then based around the corner from St James's Park in London. Sinclair knew that bombing raids would be launched, and briefly considered the idea of special underground living quarters for the codebreakers. That was dismissed in favour of the more practical idea of taking them out of London. Bletchley was just forty-five minutes away from the capital by train. It also had direct rail connections to Oxford and Cambridge, where so much of the recruiting was done.

Very quickly it became obvious that the house could not actually be used for codebreakers to sleep in because there was not enough room. Instead, the ever-expanding army of cryptologists were billeted with scores of puzzled landladies in the town and in the pretty villages all around. The landladies and all the other locals knew that the institution at the old Leon place was top secret, made obvious by the barbed wire and the sentry hut at the gate. But what was it for? Mystery piled upon mystery with some of the more outré recruits. Novelist-to-be Angus Wilson had a sense of style characterised by indigo shirts coupled with apricot-coloured bow ties that had never been seen before in a town like Bletchley. Then there were the debutantes, posh young ladies who seemed to have swept directly out of the society pages in extraordinary frocks and furs, and who caught the night express to London to go dancing in Claridges.

For the Bletchley locals who had largely only known brickmaking, the chief industry of the town, there could only be one answer to the mystery, which was that Bletchley Park had been turned into a very special secret government lunatic asylum. But what then could explain all the green-painted huts that had sprung up around the grounds? And later in the war, what significance did the specially built one-storey concrete blocks bear? The townsfolk soon realised that all the women and men working within those gates weren't mad, but they were formidable brainboxes.

At one local pub, some of the young men became regulars and whenever they wanted to discuss anything to do with their work, they suddenly switched from English to Ancient Greek. A local vicar had several young mathematicians billeted in his rectory and he could not bear the secrecy. At every available opportunity, he attempted to trick his young guests into giving a clue about what they were doing. In fact, he became so insistent that one of the young chaps thought he ought to mention it to the Park authorities. The authorities took the matter very seriously, so much so that the vicar then received a visit from an intelligence officer. Following the incident, the Park's director, Alistair Denniston, mentioned in a memo that the vicar was 'not a bad man' but a 'foolish one' and had to be given 'a fright'. The reason very simply was this: if the secret of Bletchley Park were to ever escape its gates and get out into the wider world and give the Nazis even the smallest clue that their apparently impenetrable ciphers had been wrenched wide open, the entire country's war effort could be crippled.

Because what they were achieving at the Park was quite literally crucial for the survival of the nation. By breaking into the Nazi Enigma codes, the cryptologists were fighting back against the lethal U-boats that were stalking British convoys and destroying food supplies. On top of this, the codebreakers were thwarting the aims of the Luftwaffe, and giving invaluable intelligence to the armies in the deserts of north Africa. By 1944, Bletchley Park would be crucial to the success of D-Day, decrypting Nazi messages virtually in real time to let commanders in the field know how the Germans were planning to react and retaliate. Bletchley Park was the centre of a web with threads right the way around the world, from the torrid jungles of the Far East to the ice floes of the Arctic. The thousands of women and men who worked here – the codebreakers and the debutantes joined by great platoons of Wrens – were helping to shape the future. But that success depended upon the Nazis never guessing at this triumph, for if they were to do so, then they would have doubled the complexity of their encryptions and heightened their security, making any other breakthroughs impossibly difficult for many years.

Given all that, the mostly young recruits to the Park wore this unfathomable pressure lightly, even if it took a physical toll in terms of tiredness. There were those among them who turned heads in the town for reasons other than dottiness. One operative was a well-known (and very glamorous) British film actress called Dorothy Hyson, who had co-starred with the comedian George Formby, among others. Eight-hour shifts in a blacked-out hut filled with the haze of tobacco took her into a different realm. And indeed, when her lover, the actor Anthony

Quayle, then in the Special Operations Executive, came to the town to see her, he was shocked at the dark circles under her eyes and her wan complexion. What sort of work could she have been doing to make her look so weak? But like everyone else, she was not permitted to give him even the smallest clue.

There were outlets to balance all this hard work. Any Bletchley local walking past the main gates in the insect-singing warmth of a summer's evening might have been taken aback to hear the piercing notes of an enthusiastic bagpipe band echoing down the driveway from the house coming from a gramophone. And the reason for the music was the Park's highland dancing club. The house had provision for more conventional dances as there was a ballroom, with an intact sprung floor and a decorative ceiling. Debutante Sarah Baring, who was used to weekends in much grander country houses, never cared for this space, and the carved ceiling which, she said, simply looked like 'a lot of drooping bosoms'.[26] One American codebreaker who was an architect by training described the house as having been designed in a style he called 'Lavatory Gothic'.

But the metaphorical walls between the codebreakers and the ordinary townspeople of Bletchley were frequently breached, with the secret kept carefully safe. Many of the codebreakers had great artistic talents. There were some, waiting to go on nightshifts in the summer, who would make their way down to the canal beforehand as the rosy sun began to set and sing madrigals. Then there were the variety shows which the cryptologists adored performing in. There were songs and comical sketches which would be presented to local people in the villages and towns all around in community halls. The codebreakers staged serious dramas in these halls too, including productions of plays like *They Came to a City* by J. B. Priestley. Not only would they act, but they would also build all the sets and design the costumes. The Bletchley Park players became so established in north Buckinghamshire that towards the end of the war, the local press started sending critics to give the plays and shows proper full write-ups. The critics were as curious as everyone else about the provenance of the actors but unlike the nosy vicar, they were wise enough not to speculate too far.

From the point of view of some of the recruits, though, Bletchley Park seemed very far from their idea of what a top-secret headquarters would look like. The summons to go there was satisfyingly cryptic. Sarah Baring received a telegram telling her to report to 'Station X', with directions. And indeed, for many, the late-night arrival at the railway station with blacked-out platforms wreathed in mist, the echo of steps on the iron footbridge, the roar of West Coast expresses steaming through, then the contact outside the station door, had a delicious touch of pulp thriller espionage. But then, in the daylight, as the reality of this slightly odd and dowdy-looking house, and the huts all around filled with even odder people sank in, the more sophisticated recruits compared their new surrounds ruefully to the sweepingly beautiful Oxford and Cambridge quads that they had left behind.

There were other layers of permeability as well. This was not a base that could remain wholly sealed off from the outside world. The codebreakers needed feeding, for a start, and the canteen at Bletchley Park, run by women who lived locally, was a social focal point for the hungry younger people. In severely rationed times, the food could sometimes be a revelation with varieties of fresh vegetables and meat procured from local farms. But not always, and some of the debutantes shuddered as they faced helpings of Woolton Pie (a rationing special composed chiefly of turnips and potatoes). The exception was one of Prince Philip's girlfriends; Osla Benning's appetite was so prodigious that after she finished one helping, she would slide on a pair of sunglasses and rejoin the dinner queue for seconds, pretending to be someone else. A watchful presence among all these bright young things was someone even younger, who had recently been evacuated from London with her mother. Mimi Galilee was Bletchley's youngest worker, aged fourteen. Her mother had secured herself a job in the canteen and told the Park's personnel department that her daughter was desperate to leave school so would there be anything at all that she could do around the Park? And so, Mimi Galilee became a messenger, shuttling between the big house and all the huts and observing people who, she said years later, seemed 'god-like' to her.[27] Less god-like was her big sister, who also secured a role at the Park performing clerical duties.

And among these intellects moved a figure whose name would be first erased from history and then triumphantly restored with full honour. The brilliant mathematician and philosopher Alan Turing, who was the first to envisage the modern computer and the possibilities of artificial intelligence, was not that much older than some of the students who had been pulled out of their universities. He was twenty-seven years old when he started applying his mind to the possibility of a thinking machine that could outwit the Nazis. Turing and another young thunderbolt called Gordon Welchman brought the 'Bombe' machines into being; those behemoths that taxed the patience of so many ministering Wrens. And it was Turing and Professor Max Newman who teamed up with the engineer Tommy Flowers to bring the Colossus machine into this world. For a time, Turing was the head of Hut 8, which was focused on German naval codes and he had his own methods of banishing tension. One of these was long-distance running. Turing greatly appreciated the landscape around Bletchley Park for that very reason for it gave him a chance to go haring off across fields and down the towpath of the Grand Union Canal. It was rumoured that he had once run the entire length of it down to London. Turing might have had an alternative career as a serious athlete. He could, almost without thinking about it, run a marathon in two hours and forty minutes.

In the earliest days of the institution, the Park director Alistair Denniston fretted a little about the town itself. He wondered if all his bright new recruits might find it a little drab and unexciting compared even to the blacked-out restrictions of London? This was rather unfair on Bletchley which, for a small town, offered a choice of cinemas and a department store and some wonderfully traditional pubs, such as The Shoulder of Mutton. And while some of the debutantes did indeed go dancing in Mayfair, taking care to return to the town on the 5 a.m. milk trains out of Euston, other codebreakers rather revelled in the peaceful atmosphere of the town and its surrounds. For those who had been drawn from the smog-choked big cities of Scotland and the industrial north, here was something cleaner and quainter, a mazy profusion of narrow country lanes leading to small villages and a whole range of picnicking options by bicycle on sunny days. And the Park itself with its spacious grounds offered everything from tennis to wildly competitive rounders. In the deep-frozen winters, the lake before the house naturally became a much-used ice-skating rink. Movement was very important at Bletchley after hours hunched over encrypted messages or patiently assembling the vast cross-referenced card index. So too was sunshine, especially after bright days working in blacked-out huts. After shifts, codebreakers were encouraged to lie out in the grass to soak up the much-needed vitamin D.

Even when the war ended, no one could say a word about what went on in Bletchley Park. Paperwork went up in huge bonfires, complex machinery was broken and smashed up and every last blackboard and bit of chalk were cleared out from the huts. The Colossus machines were removed (though two were not destroyed, as the rumour went, they instead found a new home in what was to become GCHQ). But even though most of the codebreakers returned to their old lives, significant figures like Hugh Alexander and Alan Turing's one-time fiancée Joan Clarke stayed on and went to Eastcote, then Cheltenham. The Park itself remained a government institution. Throughout the fifties, sixties and seventies, it was used as a telecommunications training hub and young people would go there on courses. And the ballroom with its 'drooping bosoms' ceiling found a gasp of new life as a discotheque.

But this new incarnation gradually sputtered and faded. Close by to Bletchley was the new city of Milton Keynes. Next to it, Bletchley looked rather faded and indeed a little anachronistic. By the 1990s, the house and the grounds were disused and beginning to crumble. There was serious discussion about turning the site into a vast new supermarket with attendant car park. The unloved house would be quietly demolished.

Thankfully, by this stage, the extraordinary story of the codebreakers had now flooded out into the public domain with a series of books in the 1970s and 1980s prising the lid further and further back, outlining the astounding triumph against Enigma. And there was a determined group of people who saw that the Park had to be saved as a truly historic monument. Their work was not easy because years of neglect had brought the house and many of its satellite buildings to the point of collapse. But with incredible efforts and diligence and care, the restoration was undertaken, and the Park began to receive interested paying visitors. The numbers rose, and so too did the funds for further restorations. The virtuous circle grew wider as Park veterans – who had been forbidden by the Official Secrets Act to ever discuss what they had done there – now began to return for the first time for special veteran reunions, which were always warm, emotional and laughter-filled days.

There were veterans like Jean Valentine who, in her eighties, volunteered to lead tours around the Park, giving demonstrations on reconstructed Bombe machines. She and fellow former Wren Ruth Bourne attracted their own huge followings and between them they brought ever more coach parties. They also brought royalty and the Queen visited the Park for the first time in 2012. As well as getting her chance to meet codebreakers like Keith and Mavis Batey, and Oliver and Sheila Lawn (couples who had met and fallen in love at the Park), it was noted by some that if the young Princess Elizabeth, during the war, had wished to see around Bletchley Park, she would not have been allowed, even in her position as an ATS volunteer.

This is one of the reasons why Bletchley still grips the imagination: not just because of what was achieved here, but also because of the brilliant ironies of who was and who was not allowed to know anything. James Bond's creator, Ian Fleming, who was in Naval Intelligence, knew all about it, but lower ranking MI5 or MI6 agents were kept firmly out of the loop. If 007 had been a real figure, not even he would have been allowed over the threshold of Bletchley Park.

And its best-known hero, Alan Turing, has found his proper place in the national pantheon. In the early 1950s, his homosexuality led to a conviction which – it is thought – contributed to his suicide in 1953 aged forty-two. His achievements might have remained forever in the shadows but thankfully the resurrection of Bletchley Park dovetailed with the rediscovery of his life and his impact upon computing. There is a sensitive bust of Turing at the Park. But the place is also infused with the spirit of all those who worked there, including the debutantes who pushed each other along corridors in laundry baskets and the Wrens who took full advantage of the irksomely hot Colossus machines to dry their newly washed underwear.

How to get there

Of all the landmarks in Secret Britain, Bletchley Park is the one that draws the greatest number of fascinated pilgrims, and it is not difficult to understand why. The house and huts have been rebuilt in the wartime style, with incredible faithfulness to detail, and there are a range of modern exhibits concerning codes and computers that are fascinating to old and young alike. As such, it is these days essential to book ahead. To drive, Bletchley isn't far from junction 13 of the M1. For many, railway will be the easiest option (and in its own way gives a taste of what it was like for the arriving codebreakers, even if the station was barbarically rebuilt in the 1960s). Bletchley is on the

West Coast line, and there are direct services from London and Northampton, or one can easily change from express services one stop away at Milton Keynes. The Park itself is just across the road from the railway station, if you walk along the signposted path for a few yards you will soon be at the main gate.

SECRET TUNNELS

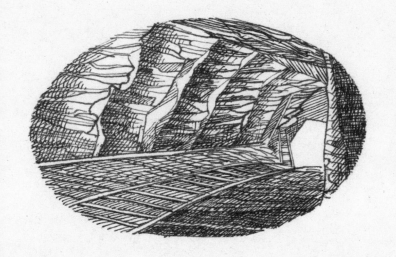

The Noises in the Dark

Easter Ross oil storage tank tunnels,
Inchindown Hill, Cromarty

There are some man-made tunnels that can overwhelm explorers with a sense of the uncanny. Where the total blackness and the curious acoustics can make the most irrational fears of the dark suddenly take on the most suffocating form. Unlike natural caves and caverns, with their echoes, their pools, their stalactites and their rocky passages which at least feel natural, a vast artificial cavern that can only be accessed via a narrow concrete pipe and a cold tunnel, that has been disused for many years, carries quite a different charge. In the very far north of Scotland, the year before the Second World War broke out, far-sighted authorities decreed that cathedral-sized vaults should be excavated beneath a hill overlooking the Cromarty Firth. In 1938, this was still a matter for manual labour rather than mechanical diggers. This was to be a secret oil storage tank almost beyond the scale of imagination and it was to be a lifeline for the battleships in the Firth and heading out into the North Sea. This was a time when it was correctly anticipated that Hitler's air forces would be attempting to target the nation's fuel supplies. As a result, the engineering achievement was extraordinary. But from the start, it was also curiously unsettling.

There were already overground tanks that had been there since the First World War. But this Admiralty-backed idea was dauntingly ambitious: six 'cells', or enormous caverns, measuring some 750 feet in length, and some 50 feet in height, could each hold five million gallons of oil. In addition to this were access tunnels and, naturally, pipelines to feed the oil down through the hills for a distance of four miles to the harbour. The project was too enormous simply for the local workforce (not least because this was and is a sparsely populated corner of the country). Starting in 1938, the engineers began bringing in workers from all over Scotland and beyond. According to accounts from relatives years later, many men were brought over from County Donegal in the north of Ireland, an echo of Victorian navvy labour on the Highland railways. The pay was not especially handsome but there were occasional bonuses (that is, for rationed times) in the form of catching rabbits and hares for delicious stews. They were encamped near the walls of Castle Dobie. The weather alone was a fearsome proposition and come the deep darkness of winter, the gales and the blizzards made bicycle journeys to and from the excavation site bitingly agonising. Nor was it that much more comfortable on the dig. Throughout the course of gouging out Inchindown Hill, the men on duty were constantly inhaling dust and the thin paper masks

The uncanny cavern: disused oil tank tunnel.

that they had been issued with were of little use. Many years later, a number of men who had worked down there suffered respiratory and related health problems. In addition, there was an ever-present danger of rockfall (there were no safety helmets, only caps and hats) and the process of removing the stony spoil from the ever-deepening caverns, which involved heaving great weights of excavated rock to the surface, was also grindingly hard. It is quite remarkable that the entire project was completed in just over two years, in 1941.

And as predicted, the bombers came, and any remaining overground oil storage facility was targeted. But the Easter Ross caverns were not only hewn from rock, they had also been lined with layers of concrete as a further means of precaution. As a piece of secret civil engineering, and unlike many other wartime structures, these cells were built to endure for a great many years to follow.

Yet from the start, they carried a lurking sense of un-ease. Many years later, relatives of those who had worked there remembered stories about the caverns acquiring a haunted reputation. This, it was suggested, was because that part of the country is suffused with prehistoric tombs, and the construction of the subterranean tanks disrupted several sacred sites. There were rumours of poltergeist activity. Ingeniously, it was also suggested that some of these stories were deliberately started by the authorities to discourage the curious from investigating the tunnels. Nonetheless, relatives of those who worked there remember that there was an awareness of the prox-imity of the longbarrows and by extension, the nearness of the long-distant dead.

But whether there were other presences in that dark-ness or not, the fact was that the tunnels were a fantastic wartime boon. In all, those caverns could home some thirty-two million gallons of oil, which meant that this was a vital harbour for the nation's warships. The locals who naturally were all perfectly well aware of what lay beneath Inchindown Hill were also perfectly canny when it came to the idea of careless talk costing lives. Curiously, just a little down the coast, there had been an espionage drama where in a tiny fishing village called Port Gordon, a man tried to buy a railway ticket at the local station with a £50 note. The stationmaster put in a discreet call to the local police and the man was arrested before the train arrived. He was indeed a German spy, and the currency was a huge and silly mistake. In a community as small and cut off as Port Gordon, £1 notes – let alone £50 notes – were rare enough as it was.

Despite potential interest from German agents, the secret of the tanks remained safe. And they were built so soundly that they were in steady use in the years after the war as well. Indeed, they played a vital part in the fuelling of the naval fleet for the 1982 Falklands conflict. It was only after this that the Easter Ross oil vaults were deemed to have reached their natural end. But they never stopped exerting their fascination over those who had heard the stories.

Just recently, photographers Simon Riddell and David Allen mounted an expedition into the tunnels to see how they might best be captured on film. Their aim was to capture one perfect shot of one of the storage vaults and develop it on site without the aid of digital technology or enhancement. The amount of time this would take meant that they also had to camp in the access tunnels over-night. Their progress was reported on BBC Scotland and the assignment was not only physically difficult but also rather unnerving. They brought equipment through the narrow passages by rolling it along on skateboards. 'I've been a firefighter so I'm no stranger to uncomfortable places,' Mr Riddell told the BBC. 'But there was one time when I wasn't very comfortable. I had to take down all the gear before Dave arrived. Something made a noise and

I just got a little bit worried. Even though you know that you are the only person there – you've locked yourself in – but you are still in this dark, black place.'[28]

Contributing to the eerie atmosphere were the extraordinary acoustics. It was reckoned at one point that the Easter Ross tunnels had the longest reverberation in the world. But as the photographers and a great many men before them found, this could also lead to a disorientating cacophony. If anyone attempted to have a conversation while standing a few feet apart from each other, their voices would rise to the vaulted roofs and bounce around the chamber in a seemingly unstoppable echo that would then drown out any further attempts to speak.

An additional disorientation might have been the rich prevalence of oil vapour in the air; although the vaults now stood high and empty, the walls and the floors retained the memory of those extraordinarily huge black pools.

There was a plan back in the 1980s that NATO would take over as the chief customer for the tanks, but this came to nothing. Eventually, the tunnels were opened up for strictly limited and guided tours. There were huge numbers of people desperate to get down into those vaults. And for a time, a few did get down there. For now, though, it seems that the tunnels are inaccessible to the general public, even to the hardiest and least claustrophobic. Yet the secret tunnels of Easter Ross remain an important, if invisible, landmark in the story of ingenious Second World War engineering, to say nothing of the preternatural strength and spirit of the men who carried out that engineering vision.

HOW TO GET THERE

The chances of getting into the tunnels now are extremely remote, unless you happen to be a television documentary maker. But the landscape around is worth taking in if you are on a Highland tour. The site is about thirty miles north of the nearest big city, Inverness, and the rich vista of hills and shouldering mountains peaked in white is quite breathtaking. This is a land where prehistory can still be felt; a region of long-barrow tombs that give the long departed warriors a proximity to the present day. But there are also the more straightforward lures of the wider area, from the site of the Culloden battlefield to Macbeth's old home of Cawdor Castle. The nearest large town to the site is Invergordon, which may be familiar to cruise passengers who have docked in its harbour for Highland tours. The town itself is an interesting mix of Scottish industry (rig maintenance) and doughty nineteenth-century stone architecture. It lies just off the A9 and there is a railway station that runs services from Inverness through to stations further north.

The Colours in the Darkness

Manod Quarry, Blaenau Ffestiniog

Imagine that you have been asked to protect just one priceless work of art, like a mesmeric Vermeer or an exquisitely detailed Rembrandt. You have been told to take that one masterpiece out of its carefully guarded gallery to somewhere many miles away, into the heart of one of the country's most mountainous regions where the gales and the rain and the snow scour the bare moors. You are not allowed to store the painting in any building with a roof. What is more, that painting will have to withstand the journey and will need to stay in this region for many years. And you will be expected to keep that painting completely pristine and unfaded and untouched by any of the ravages of climate or time. Where would you even begin? Now imagine the same proposition but with thousands of works of art, all completely beyond value in the ordinary sense. A collection including (among thousands of others) pieces by Leonardo da Vinci, Rembrandt, Constable and Gainsborough. This was the stomach-dropping challenge facing the National Gallery as the Second World War broke out. They needed to evacuate each and every one of their artistic masterpieces, including the most fragile Old Masters, and find a secret hiding place for them for the duration of the conflict. In some ways, this was about the artistic soul of the nation, and the sanctuary that was settled upon was to prove one of the most aesthetically beguiling secret locations of the entire war.

The bombers were anticipated in London. There had been a form of rehearsal for such an eventuality in 1938 when Prime Minister Neville Chamberlain had flown to Munich to negotiate with Hitler. In that instance, fifty paintings were transported from the gallery to Bangor in north Wales. When the Munich talks produced apparent 'peace in our time', they were immediately returned. The British were not the only ones making alarmed preparations. The same was true over in Nazi Germany. And the Nazis hit upon much the same sort of answer for the storage of irreplaceable masterpieces. The places where the enemy planes were hardly likely to strike were mountains. And the caverns within would be fashioned into safety deposit vaults for the most delicate of canvasses.

When the staff of the National Gallery in London were weighing up the full extent of their treasures – and the quite terrifying responsibility of shipping them all to a place of safety – they were also sending reconnaissance around the country to scout out potential subterranean spaces. It soon became apparent that a vast and forbidding slate quarry in north Wales, close to Snowdonia, would be perfect, for deep within the high quarry wall was a huge natural cavern. Of course, it would have to be adapted as the slate mine was impenetrably dark and wet, and occasionally dangerous too for those who had been working there across the years. So how could this be made a suitable home for the breathtaking work of everyone from Van Gogh to Van Dyck? And there were other tremendous logistical problems to consider too, mainly to do with transportation. How could one safely arrange for the mass evacuation of Britain's artistic heritage, first without anything getting even slightly damaged and second without anyone seeing or noticing? Security was paramount; the possible consequences of intelligence whispering back to the enemy about where precisely all this treasure lay might have resulted in the deliberate targeting of that treasure, and a shattering blow to national morale.

The Manod Slate Quarry, a little distance from the nearest town of Blaenau Ffestiniog, was not a forgiving proposition. As a working quarry, it was an extraordinarily harsh environment. Over the years, the men who came to hew the slate from the mountains were vulnerable to respiratory diseases caused by the toxic stone dust. There were also frequent accidents. It was estimated at one point that the average life expectancy of the Manod quarrymen was forty-seven years old. In addition to this, the unforgiving climate and terrain meant that the transportation of anything more delicate and precious than slate could pose a hundred knotty difficulties. This was not the sort of landscape that the more fastidious art specialists of the National Gallery were used to working in.

When war came on 3 September 1939, the evacuation of the entire gallery was affected at lightning speed. Before the Manod quarries could be made fully ready, some of the finest works of art on the planet were packed with infinite care and driven out of London to various holding locations in mid and north Wales, including the cheerful seaside gothic splendour of the National Library of Wales in Aberystwyth, the University of Bangor and Penrhyn Castle.

The Gallery's director, Kenneth Clark, would not have been short of the social connections that might have seen paintings going to many more castle walls. However, this was never a possibility, though one idea that had been discussed was sending the collection out of the country altogether, to Canada. This idea was stamped on firmly: quite apart from the distressing symbolism, the danger was intense. Transatlantic ships could be sunk all too easily. On top of this, Winston Churchill, in conversation with Clark, was adamant. 'Hide them in caves or cellars,' he said, 'but not one picture shall leave this island.'[29]

With the Manod quarry agreed upon, the slate mine and the mountain roads and railways around had to be customised to greet their lustrous new guests. To begin, the cave entrance had to be enlarged with dynamite. It had previously been an acceptable size for men to enter but vast, epic canvases needed more headroom. Within the cavern, special brick-built 'cells' that were spacious and rigorously air-conditioned were constructed as the shelter within the shelter. Here in these mini galleries, the physical state of the paintings could be checked constantly, and the temperature very carefully regulated. In addition to all of this, the narrow-gauge railway that climbed from Blaenau Ffestiniog had to be extended a little and adapted. On the roads, headroom for the larger canvases had to be addressed and the road that ran beneath one small bridge was dug and effectively lowered, so that the Gallery's traffic could pass through.

And so, the extraordinary odyssey into the mountains began in full in 1941 – under conditions of the very deepest secrecy. Of course, the people in Blaenau Ffestiniog could see that something was happening but no one could be precisely sure what. In order that the nature of the cargo be disguised, some of the world's greatest works of art started arriving in the area in Cadbury's chocolate delivery vans and what, onlookers wondered, would be the need to store chocolate high amid all the slate? That part of the quarry was now very firmly under the direct control of Whitehall. For the custodians of the art, there were a great many hair-raising and wince-inducing moments as the carefully packaged works wove and wound their way to the mine entrance.

Van Dyck's 'King Charles on Horseback' – a canvas measuring twelve feet high by six feet wide – proved an especially vexatious work. At one point, the tyres of the truck carrying it had to be deflated to let it pass beneath an especially tight bridge. The man in charge of bringing the science of preservation to all these great works was the Minister of Works, Richard Meirion Jones. It was one of the pleasing ironies of the war that he did such a brilliant job in caretaking the masterpieces, with such innovative use of air control and humidity regulation, that the Gallery picked up invaluable tips for its own display rooms for when the paintings would be safely restored. Yet the slate mine repository was also one of the secret war's most surreal images: the starkly lit caverns, the small railway trailing through this labyrinth, the dark jagged walls, and all around, the men in tweed with pipes and glasses, checking thermometers and pulling agonised faces at the prospect of moving any of their limitlessly beautiful treasures.

But the entire exercise was so effective that as the war ended and the equally careful operation to remove these thousands of paintings and restore them to the National Gallery got underway, Clement Attlee's post-war government decided to hold on to the slate mine. In a new and nervy era and in a time in which war could easily have come again, it made sense not to let go of what had been the most brilliant Aladdin's Cave, just in case it was needed once more. The secrecy remained absolute. Some years later, there was a dress rehearsal for another even speedier art evacuation, this time in response to the possibility of nuclear strikes. On this occasion, copies of the real things were used and they came in great convoys up to the mountain and back into that mine with those still-standing brick bungalows. The reason for the secrecy in the nuclear age was in a way rawer than that of the war; it was that if the general public – either in London

*Hidden glory: the techniques developed in the Manod Caverns
to preserve masterpieces were used after the war.*

or in Blaenau Ffestiniog – realised that the nation's art was
being hidden away at speed, then there was a possibility
that a mass panic could be sparked.

As it was, there was never again a need to hide away
the fine art pieces, but the mines of Manod remained in
the hands of Whitehall until the early 1980s. In all those
decades, not a syllable about their real use had seeped
out into the wider community and this meant that in this
particular region of north Wales, the rumours about what
the government might be keeping in those old slate mines
were outlandish.

There are now other reasons for the public being kept away from the caverns which are to do with physical safety as opposed to stashed Old Masters. Yet it is worth pondering – in the event of any conflict in the far future – whether the maze of caves might be pressed into use once more.

HOW TO GET THERE

While the exact caverns are now difficult to get to, the area around Blaenau Ffestiniog is alive with a whole range of activities that make the fullest use of its heritage of slate. There are quarry tours that take you deep into other nearby slate mines, far underground, with their sometimes ghoulish histories related faithfully. For those who worked there one hundred years ago and more, life was inconceivably tough. But the tours will also give an idea of air temperature and humidity, and all the other factors entwined in art preservation. The area also abounds in zip wires and furiously fast mountain-bike trails, as well as spectacular walks, with the dark mountains looming in the distance. What was once one of the remotest corners of the country has become one of the most sought-after in terms of visitors. Blaenau Ffestiniog (the Manod quarries tower a couple of miles outside of the town) is on the A470 and the A496. There is also a railway terminus and one can catch a train from Llandudno Junction to Blaenau where there are several services a day. There is also the famous attraction of the narrow-gauge Blaenau Ffestiniog railway, a steam train summer treat.

No Naked Flames

Rhydymwyn Tunnels, Mold

There were some secrets hidden under the ground that were too dark to be spoken of – the obscene precautions taken for total war involving civilians. Unlike stored art, or fuel lagoons, there was a series of tunnels on the Welsh border that contained something that no nation would ever willingly admit to having stockpiled. This was a substance that had to be treated with the most terrible care. And this secret was vital to keep because it would have been nightmarishly easy for a saboteur to create havoc on a dreadful scale. Throughout the war, those who worked in these echoing tunnels were continually watched by pairs of careful observers. No man could be entirely trusted around what they had down here. More than this, the technical logistics involved in getting the substance into the vaults in the first place was fraught. Even if the local people had an inkling of what was going on in the freshly dug Rhydymwyn Tunnels, they knew as if by instinct that this was not a subject for excitable gossip or hilarious rumours. Instead, there was a leaden seriousness about the site.

Here was where supplies of mustard gas were being stored, after being manufactured in the factory above and at sites elsewhere. The nightmare of the previous conflict, that poisoned and blinded so many in the trenches, was being made again. The idea was that if the Nazis should attempt to deploy it, Britain would be able to retaliate. Here was the first inkling of the total war to come. In the end, fire was the chosen weapon to be dropped on residential areas in the forms of incendiaries and explosives. Yet the stockpiling of mustard gas was a sign of the nihilism directly provoked by Nazism, itself a cult of death. Those who worked in the tunnels and the factory above noted that – unlike other similar facilities – there was a particular silence and solemnity about this one, most markedly on the night shifts. The mustard gas was contained in a range of different casings and canisters, and indeed bomb casings. To get the substance into any container was a matter of lethal precision, and there were, according to one who worked there, a lot of accidents. There was no indication of any plans for deployment of this chemical weapon, but it had to be maintained with extreme care. Men and women alike worked on the site, most of whom were drawn from the local area. They were taken to their shifts on a double-decker bus. And the women especially did not care for the night shifts.

That such a tranquil and gentle green landscape, tucked deep into a valley in a corner of north Wales not very far from Chester, could host such a sinister proposition would have seemed wholly unlikely to prying eyes.

The tunnels themselves were straightforward concrete affairs, driven through the secure limestone, after some local waterways had been diverted. And the structure was punctuated with storage bays for thousands of large canisters. But it always seemed to be damp. And for some of those working there, spraying the mustard gas canisters with various coded colours or testing them for leakages, there was one perennial nuisance: bats. The creatures found the warm artificial depths exceptionally congenial. One woman interviewed years later by the Rhydymwyn Valley History Society, remembered that there was the ever-present threat of getting bats caught in her hair; this also added to the faintly gothic atmosphere of the tunnels. Another woman worker remembered how when she was wheeling hardware along to the end of tunnel sections, she became oppressively aware of the shadows and the dark; with the only other sound that of the echoing footsteps of others, it was easy to fall into a constant state of unease.

The chemical weapons were not the only deadly secrets on this site; elsewhere there were the beginnings of experimental research into the first atomic bomb. While laboratories at Euston (see 'The Nuclear Terminus and the Soviet Spy', p. 95) were more focused on the theoretical side, specialist equipment was set up in Rhydymwyn, far away from the most inquisitive eyes. Working here for a time overseeing these physics experiments was a young scientist called Klaus Fuchs, who would later be sent to America to work on the US atomic weapons programme known as the Manhattan Project.

He also happened to be an agent for the Soviet Union. Since throughout the war Stalin was, strictly speaking, an ally, then Fuchs might have reasoned that passing the most incredibly confidential atomic secrets to the Soviets could not be counted as treachery. Yet the very fact of this terrible intelligence being dispersed into a wider world made it automatically dangerous, for what was to stop the Nazis successfully spying upon the Russians?

The local men and women who worked here were unaware of this dimension of the tunnels and the plain brick factories; the hazard of the mustard gas was quite enough to be going along with. The wider local community also sensed that the tunnels contained nothing wholesome, since there were occasional official warnings concerning what to do in the event of a 'gas escape'. Some who lived nearby only knew for certain that the tunnels contained 'nasty things'[30]; this even though the expertise was partly provided by the corporate household name of ICI. The facilities in the tunnels and the factories included showers so that at the end of shifts overalls could be discarded for cleaning and decontamination, while workers thoroughly scrubbed themselves. There were a range of other precautions. One woman who worked as a bomb supervisor recalled that the tunnel floors were made of asphalt rather than concrete: this was because they had to be completely, utterly smooth for these mustard-gas bombs to be pushed along on trolleys. Not even the slightest jolt could be risked. There were also on-site chemists who were experts at detecting and dealing with problems.

One young man who worked deep in the facilities for a time remembered the laboratories and the even more stringent safety rules after handling the toxic materials. There was special clothing (such as jackets made of rough material and without lapels), the careful demarcation of toxic and non-toxic zones and the chemicals required to decontaminate instruments and human flesh. There were also police on-site who were unobtrusive but ever present. The opportunities such materials could present to saboteurs were endless.

Yet despite the grim nature of the work where, unlike other wartime factories, there was strictly no music on site and no cheering tunes from radio shows like *Workers' Playtime*, because no distractions could be allowed, the life outside the tunnels was for many rather congenial. Large numbers of the workers were bussed in from the pretty local market town of Mold, which itself was equipped with a range of possibilities for escapism. There were local cinemas, local dances, busy pubs and also fantastic walking trails for local ramblers. In the end, so much is about adaptability and for the young people of the tunnels working bravely with the most insidious and deadly substances and knowing precisely what these bombs were for, there could be not even the slightest shade of romanticism about the war. This was a tough location that required all its recruits to stare at the more uncomfortable aspects of war morality head on.

Nor was there any apparent shift in that stance with victory in Europe. Most of the young people were demobilised and free to go off and pursue their peacetime careers but the mustard gas remained in the tunnels for some years afterwards. In a new atomic age of the Cold War, it was looking as barbarous and as outdated as the rack. It is difficult to conceive of any circumstances under which its use might even be threatened. Equally, it was not an easy substance to dispose of safely and it was not until 1959 that the long-defused bombs and their poison essences were dispersed. Various governments still found other industrial purposes for the site but by the early 1990s, the tunnels were cleared of all equipment and the factory sites above became derelict. And it was only then that the original purpose of the site began to emerge from the deep shadows of secrecy.

Those who worked there recalled how very cold the tunnels were. This did nothing to discourage brilliant local chroniclers such as Colin Barber, who explored the now empty site, and carefully put together the mosaic of what had once been a secret history. The area remains tucked away; it is a part of the world that seems in its own way as off the beaten track as certain regions of Scotland. Therein of course lies an entire world of charm. A corner of the country where the most beautiful landscapes begin to be punctuated the closer to the Mersey you get with fascinating industry. The tunnels of Rhydymwyn were as sombre a prospect as it was possible to get and those who have joined recent tours of the site will have come away with that chilled sense of the cold reality of war.

How to get there

The nearest town, several miles away, is Mold, which lies on the junction of several roads, and Mold itself is a few miles away from the much larger town of Chester. It is not on the railway but if you are staying overnight at Mold, it might be worth changing at Chester, getting a train to Flint, or Buckley a little further south, and hiring a cab from there.

The Tunnels that Breathed

Drakelow Tunnels, near Kidderminster

On one terrible night in November 1940, the Luftwaffe flew over the Midlands town of Coventry and by showering it with incendiaries and high explosives, reduced the historic timber-framed city centre to glowing ash. The infernal heat was so intense that lead piping melted and ran in seething molten rivulets into the gutters. The sandstone of the medieval beauty of Coventry Cathedral became luminous on that cold night, a terrifying and intense ruby light in the darkness. The bombers were attempting to raise a firestorm in a hideous phenomenon of physics that caused flames from burning buildings to join with one another and in so doing, rise further and further into the sky, sucking in all the cold oxygen and whirling like a tornado. Anyone standing too close to such a monstrous quirk of nature would be pulled off the ground high into the sky, into a centrifugal tunnel of pure flame and they would be burnt alive as they flew. The targets of the Luftwaffe were British factories, the assembly lines upon which new tanks and aeroplanes were being moulded. In time, the RAF would turn this bombing campaign back upon the Nazis, flying missions deeper and deeper into the dark industrial heart of their country. More firestorms were to follow. Both the Nazis and the British faced the same icy logic problem: how would it be possible to build vast aeroplanes invisibly?

And across those manufacturing heartlands the shadow factories began to materialise; that is, production lines assembled beneath the earth, protected by blast-proof concrete, beyond the range of even the sharpest-eyed bomb aimer.

It was outside Kidderminster, twenty miles west of the mighty complex of factories and workshops and towering chimneys of Birmingham, that the local sandstone yielded to the diggers' picks. Work began in June 1941, as the Luftwaffe were criss-crossing the country, seeking to destroy everything from ports to power stations. Given that the site beneath a hill was some 250,000 square feet and stretched in total to about three and a half miles, this maze of tunnels, large enough to accommodate the most intense work, was impressively completed by 1943. It was devoted to the Bristol Aeroplane Company, which was putting together ever faster, better designed fighters and bombers. It was here that engines were made, among them the Pegasus, the Centaur and the Hercules. These engines would be fitted into (among others) Beaufighters, Halifaxes and Lancasters. Other elements of the aeroplanes first found life here too. The idea was that the components would be made here and then, in the final stage of the process, taken elsewhere to be put together in

Benignly haunted: Drakelow Tunnels, a former Second World War
shadow factory used to make military plane engine components
for the Bristol Hercules and Rolls-Royce Pegasus engines.

the manner of a jigsaw puzzle. The workforce, comprising some 700 employees from nearby Rover plants, had to adjust to a new subterranean existence. But the authorities tried to make it as easy for them as possible. In the heart of the tunnel complex was a fully fitted canteen, serving hot, freshly prepared, varied meals around the clock. The cooks there were rolling pastry, baking meats and boiling the vegetables for the many factory workers to enjoy. And alongside this, in each tunnel near each production line there were liberal numbers of lavatories, with the idea being that no worker should face the discomfort of having to trail through yards of winding tunnel trying to find the facilities.

The sandstone rock of the tunnels was lined in some strategic places with steel, another unnoticed innovation of the structure. This was nothing to do with the danger of bombs from above, but the more insidious peril of the effects of high industrial heat within the complex. If left unprotected, the stone walls of the tunnels could have subtly changed and expanded in searing temperatures, and then reverted to their old configuration as the air cooled. This in turn might have introduced a dangerous instability to the tunnels and meant that there was a chance that the workers could be crushed in deadly rock-falls. The steel lining gave the tunnels the striking ability to breathe, as though they were alive. In addition, some of the underground factory floors were specially treated, to be made acid-proof.

A young woman called Mary Cartwright, aged twenty in 1943, was called up for duties in the tunnels and she found herself placed in a scientific position where she analysed the metals that were about to be used in various components, to make sure that there were no flaws or fatigue. She had no training as an industrial chemist. 'My sister-in-law just gave me a book which told me how to do it and I just got on with it,' said Mrs Cartwright, interviewed decades later. 'The metal would come in and one of the men would drill it into shavings. I would dissolve it in acid and then . . . analyse it so I could discover how much nickel and chrome etc was in each part.'[31]

This had not been quite Mary Cartwright's wartime aim as she had wanted to go into the army. It was her parents that insisted that industry needed her more and, as she pointed out, parents had genuine authority at that time. And yet for all the absence of sunlight, and the continual noise and the other rather fiddly jobs such as subjecting the various metals to special photographic procedures for further checking, Mary Cartwright ended up relishing this unusual contribution to the war effort. 'All my memories are of a bustling hive of activity,' she recalled. 'I did enjoy my time there; it was certainly an experience. I just got on with it.'

And as soon as the war ended, the tunnels found a new purpose, this time as a ready-made factory for tank parts, because while the conflict was over, the army still needed fresh supplies of equipment for defence and deployment in a range of different countries and different situations. This continued for a while, but then the use of the tunnels changed again in 1961 and their new purpose was markedly darker. This was now a world haunted by the prospect of devastating nuclear war with the country and the landscape dying beneath a toxic fog of radiation. The grimmest contingencies had to be made and the Drakelow Tunnels were selected as one of a nationwide link of shelters that would house whatever remained of the governing authorities. What had been secret during the war now became even more unmentionable. None but a few were to know the purpose of the new blast-proof doors.

The city beneath the hill was fitted with vast water reservoirs which would be enough to keep its sheltering troglodyte population in fresh supplies for some weeks. The kitchens and the lavatories were updated, and as the years went on, so too were the communications. It was from here that officials would broadcast instructions to whoever survived the nightmare holocaust: those who could still tune radios far away from the incinerated city centres. These survivors would listen out for the grave words issued by a civil servant sitting in an incongruously floral-patterned office chair which was one of the weirdly mismatching accessories chosen for this Doomsday Base.

Thankfully, this international cloud of fear was to pass and in the 1990s, the Drakelow Tunnels were essentially abandoned. Their whispered existence – large enough numbers of people had worked there in its wartime heyday for the complex to be known locally – reached the ears of urban explorers who found various ingenious ways of gaining access to what had once been an impenetrable site. With some wonder, they explored the long miles of tunnels, bringing back both atmospheric photographs and some terrific ghost stories. One involved a solitary explorer walking through the tunnels, guided by torch, ears filled with the silence, until suddenly he could hear from an adjacent tunnel the faint sound of 1940s music. Thinking he must have company, the explorer followed the noise, which increased in volume, until he finally thought he must be upon it. He turned a corner, expecting to see people and a CD player but there was nothing there.

Nor was there anything to be heard. Puzzled, the explorer moved away and as he did so, the music began again, behind him. And this time he did not feel so inclined to find out which chamber it was coming from.

As supernatural tales go, it is almost preposterously benign, especially when you imagine these happy ghosts of Drakelow listening to the songs of Gracie Fields. It also says something for the apparently good-quality working conditions of the time. But it is also the sort of silly lure that continues to exert fascination to this day. Because the tunnels and the huge ventilation systems are now in a delicate state of repair, official visitors are few and far between. But its history remains a fine example of wartime pragmatism; the same pragmatism that in London saw the unfinished Central Line tube extension to Newbury Park being turned into a vast, thin munitions factory.

How to get there

The main entrance to the tunnels lies some five miles to the north of Kidderminster. Follow the A442 and then turn off on the B1489 and left again towards Kinver. By rail, Kidderminster station has frequent services to Birmingham, Great Malvern, and daily services to London. Some private tours of the tunnels are available and to find those most suited to your tastes (i.e. some are focused entirely upon the 'haunted' tunnels and all their possibilities of 'pure terror', which you might find a shade frenetic for your gentle historical curiosity), consult with a quick Google search of 'Drakelow tunnel tours'. Incidentally, if you have succeeded in getting through those doors, but equally want to make an entire day of it in the area, the Bodenham Arboretum, featuring 3,000 varieties of trees and shrubs, lies very close by. It is always interesting to imagine heavy industry in close proximity to such flourishing natural beauty.

The Killers in the Earth

Coed Coesau Operations Base, near Cardiff

Had the Nazis succeeded in invading and overrunning the country, who would be among the last bastions of defence, fighting on ruthlessly through espionage and sabotage and operating so far undercover that they might never be detected? While the older men of the Home Guard (portrayed with such lethal affection in the long-running BBC comedy *Dad's Army*) were more ruthless than popular memory suggests (see 'The Nazi Invasion of Birmingham', p. 102), in 1940 it was felt in Whitehall with some urgency that there had to be an elite force of trained killers standing behind them. These would be men in Home Guard uniform with a more finely sharpened expertise in the grim art of slaying the enemy. This force would come to be known, in War Office circles, as 'Churchill's Secret Army'. More officially, these small groups formed right the way across the country were known as the Auxiliary Units. They went by another nickname: the Scallywags. This had a flavour of a boys' comic strip and a suggestion of cheerful mischief. Yet with all their armaments, their brilliantly disguised explosives and their ruthless ability in hand-to-hand combat, these men stood for the absolute opposite of mischief. And the miniature underground bases for these men – again, the sorts of bunkers that would have appealed enormously to adventure-hungry children – were symbols of the grimmest intent. Huge numbers of these tiny secret underground bases remain dotted around the countryside, and not long ago, an interesting example was unearthed in south Wales between Cardiff and Caerphilly.

It lay, and still lies, in a forest. And the structure, although fashioned from concrete, has an echo of Neolithic tombs. For once you plunge within an entrance that can be slid back, you are in a claustrophobic space that to the uninformed eye is a dead end, but in fact is the first of two chambers. The reception chamber would have been roughly littered with what looked like poacher's equipment, so that if it was ever discovered, the enemy would not think of investigating any further. Beyond an interior concealed entrance lay a further chamber and this was the space in which the wireless specialist would be communicating with other secret auxiliary groups. In other bunkers (some of which, like those in the Scottish borders, were much larger and had further chambers yet for bunk beds and provisions), similar ruses to disguise the structures were used. Forest floors of moss and earth and weeds were brilliant to hide the concrete entrances. And the very quietness of these settings among the trees meant that any approaching enemy might be more easily detected. Nonetheless, the circumstances under which it was envisaged that these tunnels would be used would have been of scant comfort to the men who had trained for that moment. To be part of such an intense and aggressive resistance movement would have carried the perpetual threat of capture, agonising torture and horrifically drawn-out death. The curious and incongruous sense of security conjured by these forest-floor warrens could never have lasted long.

And unlike all the war films and boys' comics that came in the immediate aftermath of the conflict – a kaleidoscope of Spitfires and warships and the astounding undertaking of D-Day – these tunnels now also hint at the nation's more ruthless side. The men of the Auxiliary Units were very well prepared for cataclysm and were equally ready to spark off as much destruction in retaliation as they could. In the event of an emergency, the bunker at Coed Coesau was designed to be able to accommodate eight men. To supplement the minimal tinned supplies kept down there, they would have been taught the arts of foraging and hunting, emerging at night to gather what they could from the forest. The positioning of this particular bunker was key as the forest was on a sufficient elevation to allow the men to see out over the Bristol Channel and from here there would be clear radio signalling. There were lots of houses not very far away, giving a greater chance to send warning signals to other secret cells. And in addition to all of this, it lay close to a great deal of the mighty industry of south Wales, from the vast steelworks to the bustling shipping yards. These would be perennial targets for lethal sabotage and there could be no compunction.

It was Colonel John Gubbins of the Special Operations Executive who started pulling these units together in 1940 as the Battle of Britain was being fought, and the scale and reach of Hitler's intentions for Britain were assumed to be those of complete invasion and conquest. That the recruits had to be unusually tough was a given, but many were drawn from the ranks of farmers because they also needed to be in tune with living off the land. Recruitment was frequently done through word of mouth and the secret candidates were invited to Coleshill House in Wiltshire for short sharp induction courses. Amid the various skills imparted was that of assassination. This would be a cohort of agents working alongside but not with the regular troops. And they were instructed that in the event of being cornered by the enemy, the only possibility of release lay in them shooting themselves.

And very quickly the nation's woodlands came to be peppered with the brilliant camouflaged underground bases of these units. Each Auxiliary Unit was expected to look after an area of some fifteen miles radius. The Royal Engineers gave them bunkers that were also fitted with discreet observation posts and indeed alternative emergency tunnel exits should the main entrances ever be discovered. Around the country, some 500 of these small secret concrete bases were dug out. To this day, from Sussex to Ayrshire, fresh bunkers are being unearthed, sometimes because old woodlands are being cleared and sometimes because of new environmental projects. Not long ago, a Scallywag bunker was accidentally discovered in a rural location close to Edinburgh and there were still tiny indications of discarded cans and bedding that suggested it had at least been used in some form of training rehearsal.

Because of the secrecy of the Scallywags, and their hidden bunkers, a great number of those bunkers remain concealed to this day. Perhaps, in hundreds of years' time when finally they are disclosed by the changing landscape, the people will wonder if some twentieth-century men chose to live in burial chambers. As to the Scallywags themselves though, since all prospects of a Nazi invasion diminished sharply after the winter of 1940, they maintained their double Home Guard duties, with their colleagues not guessing the full deadly extent of their training. And come D-Day, a great number of the courageous Scallywags were among the thousands of men jumping ashore to face the enemy fire on those French beaches. Perhaps the bunkers can now serve as a lateral form of memorial.

HOW TO GET THERE

The Coed Coesau bunker is well signposted and lies within some deeply lovely woodland, with exhilarating views of the sea in the distance. You will not be alone as the area is fantastically popular with walkers and cyclists alike. By car you can follow the Rudry Road a few miles north out of Cardiff heading towards Coed Coesau-Whips woods. The area also lies just several miles to the east of Caerphilly. Both Cardiff Central and Caerphilly have frequent services by train.

The Ghost Stations

*Brompton Road and Down Road – former
underground stations, London*

The clay beneath the capital is seamed with an unfathomably vast and complex maze of tunnels: sewers, communications and one of the world's most extensive underground railway networks. In addition to these uncountable miles of passageways, junctions, great stretches of tube line, as well as the cathedral-like grandeur of the brick crypts through which the capital's submerged rivers run, there are also the gripping secrets. Down here, historic tunnels were dug out for clandestine purposes and there are some subterranean citadels that are still in use today. The best known of all these Second World War underground complexes are Churchill's cabinet war rooms, located beneath Horse Guards Parade, and which have been brilliantly restored and recreated for modern visitors to glean just an inkling of what it must have been like amid the ceaseless activity and with the resonant and sombre booms from above as the Luftwaffe bombs fell. Naturally the below-ground complex did not end there and there were corridors that linked along the length of

Whitehall, from the Foreign Office to the Ministry of Defence, right up to Trafalgar Square, where a secret door would allow movement to and from the Bakerloo Line underground station. For the general public, meanwhile, the authorities had excavated the epic Deep Shelters at Camden in the north and Clapham in the south. These were, as the name suggested, so far beneath the ground that the frightened population of those areas might find a little solace. In later years, these Deep Shelters found multiple fresh uses, including for the storage of sensitive Cold War material, unwelcoming temporary accommodation for some Windrush arrivals, a location for the BBC's science-fiction serial *Doctor Who* and more recently, at Clapham, as a pioneering subterranean farm.

Throughout the Blitz of 1940 and 1941, thousands of desperate Londoners bedded down in the regular tube stations, on the platforms, rather to the initial despair of the authorities. There was a fear that a great many of the public would choose simply to stay there for the duration of the war. But then there were other, irregular tube stations that were put to more direct military use. These were stations that had, a few years previously, been closed due to low passenger numbers. One such was in Knightsbridge, just a few steps away from Harrods department store and the catholic Oratory. This was Brompton Road tube station. The frontage that featured the trademark elegant ox-blood tiling of Leslie Green was still in evidence but everything that happened beneath its surface was now secret and very much off-limits to the public. This became one of the nodes of the war effort, and all just a few yards away from the daily roar of passing Piccadilly Line trains. It was from here that London's anti-aircraft artillery defences were co-ordinated.

Down the station's spiral staircase, through passages still featuring years-old cinema posters and into the musty depths, there was a drill hall, rooms for quarters, and a central control room. From here intelligence about anti-aircraft positions around the capital was collated, analysed and acted upon. The Royal Artillery covered that control room with vast maps of the city. The station was converted in other ingenious ways. The original infrastructure had featured large passenger lifts the size of small rooms, and with these no longer being necessary,

Defence of the realm: the secret life of Brompton Road tube.

the bottom of those lift shafts themselves were converted to offices. Meanwhile, the station passages still led to the old, darkened platforms and Piccadilly Line passengers could still glimpse the gleaming tiling as their trains now rushed through, towards Knightsbridge or South Kensington. For the war, a little discretion was exercised, the station platform was lowered and a brick wall then built along the length of its edge, creating more room for well-lit workspace, but keeping it carefully from the eyes of the daily travellers.

And with these spaces came other additions too, such as proper lavatories, basic kitchen units and special new air-pressure doors, designed to withstand large blasts. The control room itself was carefully lined with new tiles, which had the effect of muffling any noise from outside, and indeed the constant rumble of the trains. In addition, all the usual echoes associated with underground stations was blocked out. The result was that this curiously became one of the quietest places in London. Brompton Road underground station was also – for a time, at the height of the Luftwaffe Blitz – one of the most crucial sites in the capital too.

After the war, the tube station was never going to reopen, and so the Ministry of Defence held on to the site, putting it to a variety of different uses. Until just recently, the rooms above in the actual street-level station, including a drill hall, have been the muster point for University of London students who are attached to various wings of the RAF reserves. There were also news reports that the entire site has been sold into private hands for potential development into a huge tourist attraction. It would be easy to see such a thing working, not least because in amid the scraps of surviving war clutter underground, the station is still wonderfully rich in original signage and tiling with the elegance of the very early years of the London underground, first plunged into the darkness of secrecy and now revealed as being perfectly preserved.

The same is true of its ghost twin, also converted to a labyrinth of secret tunnels in the war. Down Street is just a mile and a half or so east and on the Piccadilly Line. It lies between Hyde Park Corner and Green Park stations and once again, at street level, one might glimpse the vestiges of that rich Arts and Crafts tiling style. But this tube station – which, like Brompton Road, was closed to passengers in the 1930s – found a rather grander secret life than its counterpart. The complex that was constructed alongside those tube rails here was frequented often by Winston Churchill and was rather more expansive and lavish in terms of office and accommodation conversions.

Nominally Down Street had been created as a sub-terranean HQ for the Executive Railway Committee, which was the body in charge of Britain's entire network throughout the war, and which had the complex role of co-ordinating troop trains and vital freight services, at a time when bombers were specifically following the silvery line of the rails beneath their flight paths. There had been an earlier site mooted before the war near Parliament but it was felt to be insufficiently secret, and thus vulnerable to a targeted attack, and also too close to the Thames to be a sensible subterranean location. Down Street in the heart of Mayfair was the solution.

And a formidable base it proved to be once the ingenious architects had converted the station. Here was not only a central control room, and all the requisite conveniences, but there was also a typing room, conference rooms and cosy sleeping quarters for up to several dozen people. There was even a large bathtub in a separate annexe. In time, this tub came to receive a particularly distinguished visitor. The rooms, furnished by the same teams that provided the seating and upholstery for the nation's trains, were given a certain stylish elegance that could apparently feel akin to being on a cruise ship.

Corridors of power: disused Down Street station.

An even more stylish feature was the entrance that VIPs could theoretically make (though it is difficult to tell if many did) rather than using the street-level frontage. The complex was designed in such a way that one could take a Piccadilly Line train – riding in the driver's cab – and stop at Down Street without any of the other passengers noticing anything untoward; there was a small and discreet gap left at the end of the bricked-over platform to allow entrance from the tunnel side. This also worked the other way around. It was possible for senior staff to 'hail' trains by means of a special red indicator. Again, they would climb into the driver's front cab while escaping the gaze of others, who would simply assume that the train was stopping in the tunnel for routine signalling reasons.

It took very little time for Churchill to learn of the wonder of the Down Street complex and though he was not personally anxious in the least about shelter throughout the Blitz – quite the reverse – he did understand that he needed a bolthole where he could sleep easily away from the general hubbub. This was such a sanctuary, not so much somewhere to hide, but somewhere peaceful to gather thoughts and also, crucially, to grab undisturbed rest.

And there were stories that Churchill's wife soon discovered the complex for herself, and indeed used the red signal on the platform as an unostentatious means of travelling to more central stations, in order to visit and talk to sheltering Londoners bedding down on the platforms. And in the meantime, the Railway Executive

Committee continued to meet throughout the war in this space which to some became a home from home. It had a pleasing incongruity with the blend of elegant refitting and old-tube-station iconography that in a way suggested continuity and a weird familiarity.

As peace came to Europe in May 1945, the Down Street complex was rendered wholly redundant and unlike the Deep Shelters, it did not immediately suggest itself for other uses such as high-security storage. And so, the station's old obsolete identity began to reassert itself, with only the unglamorous indicators of its wartime role like the lavatories and cracked sinks remaining. It became the stuff of urban legend – Piccadilly Line passengers knew the point at which to look out of the window to see where the station had once been (something similar used to happen on the Central Line between White City and Shepherd's Bush, where it was possible to make out the platform of the disused Wood Lane, and the ancient advertising posters that remained on its walls).

Elsewhere, one of the capital's Deep Shelters, one that saw very little in the way of civilians as the war progressed, lay close to the Northern Line station of Goodge Street. Here, some 100 feet underground, General Eisenhower set up a shelter HQ from which it was possible to monitor and direct subordinates above. In 1944, the point at which the Nazis were unleashing the V-1 missiles and close to perfecting the V-2 rockets, all of which were supposed to be aimed directly at the heart of the capital, Eisenhower needed a location where he could remain steadily and uninterrupted as all manner of possible carnage rained down above his head. Like Churchill, Eisenhower may have found this customised shelter conducive to focused thought.

A rather more hi-tech proposition took shape a little further east beneath the teeming streets of High Holborn. A maze of tunnels so dense that they came to be known as a 'citadel' in their own right were constructed near the Central Line, rather like the Deep Shelters running parallel and beneath the Northern Line. And like them, it was originally intended as sanctuary for Londoners from the fiery onslaught of bombing raids. But pretty soon this central underground city was marked out for a variety of other uses. Prominent among them was serving as a form of temporary headquarters for the Special Operations Executive. While their agents were out across the sea 'setting Europe ablaze', the masterminds who devised their weaponry, such as bomb detonators disguised as tree branches, and concocted their brilliantly opaque codes were often to be found down in these very well-lit depths. Here too were telephone exchanges and long corridors filled with cables and electrical machinery. There were various discreet entrances connecting with the office blocks on the streets above and also a doorway that led directly through to Chancery Lane station.

But it was the postwar afterlife of the Holborn tunnels that made it the centre of a hundred urban conspiracy theories, ranging from MI5 and MI6 secrets to the idea of an entire underground city, its people living deep in the subterranean shadows. Quite straightforwardly, it came to be used first as an overspill repository for the ever-expanding Public Records Office (which itself was much later moved out to Kew), then the tunnels underwent some conversion as part of Cold War precaution strategy. Here, aside from other uses, was where some transatlantic communications cabling was safely secured. The tunnels, a secret during the war, somehow became even more of a secret afterwards. By the 1970s and 1980s, journalists such as Duncan Campbell were following clues, such as a doorway in a certain street that appeared to lead deep down into the darkness. But there was never anything eerie about the Holborn complex – the spacious passages and the outbreaks of flashing control panels meant that it was a long way in atmosphere from the abandoned tube stations.

Even now, forgotten tunnels are being rediscovered all over the subterranean city. And even the 2,000-year-old Roman Temple of Mithras, buried deep in the London clay for centuries near to where Mansion House stands, and brought to light in the 1950s during Blitz reconstruction, has found a freshly restored cavern for a home, close to Guildhall. During the war, tunnels became an accepted backdrop for the fraught night-times, from Henry Moore sketching the citizens trying to sleep on the platforms, to the BBC's own suite of underground passages that ran beneath Broadcasting House. From the Post Office railway, running from Clerkenwell to Paddington, keeping postal deliveries running even through the bloody chaos of the

Blitz, to the passages of Downing Street's war rooms, a maze through which one could twist and turn and either find oneself within the Admiralty, or on the other side of Westminster Abbey, these subterranean passages became like the city's veins. Life moved strongly within. One young debutante called Sarah Norton, seconded to work at the Admiralty, was lost one night in the small hours within the corridors and who else should she run into but the Prime Minister himself, dressed in a magnificent scarlet dressing gown, and prowling in thought. Beneath the ground, old hierarchies could be upended.

How to get there

After years of tempting the capital's more intrepid explorers and trespassers, many of London's previously forbidden tunnels are now finding new life with special tours. The most popular (and thus, least secret) are the Cabinet War Rooms, close to Westminster underground station. But it is also possible, via booking with the London Transport Museum, to go on a tour of Down Street station. Although it is rather more ghostly than the days of its wartime splendour, it still makes for a fascinating insight into the quirks and privations of subterranean life. The nearest (working) tube station is Green Park.

SECRET CONTROL ROOMS

The Guardians of the Waves

Western Approaches Control Room and Tunnels,
Liverpool

The enemy prowled the darkest depths, while above, the ships pushing through the vast grey waves were kept in a state of permanent dread. The crews were always alert but frequently there was little they could do. By day and by night, their stalkers were invisible. Their own instruments were of some use in detection, but defence was often lacking. The ships were frequently laden with food and sailing from the United States to wartime Britain with essential supplies of staples. Britain did not have the land or the resources to feed itself. And so, these convoys of ships, churning deliberately erratic routes through storm-thrashed waters, the better to confuse and evade their pursuers, were the means by which the country could keep fighting. There were other strategies deployed to avoid the lethal attentions of the U-boat submarines, and they were needed. The U-boats could strike with torpedoes out of nowhere, ruthlessly sinking the vastest cruisers and leaving hundreds of sailors to die grim air-gulping deaths in frozen waters. Even just to stand on the deck of one of these ships on a winter's night could bring ice to eyebrows. To be plunged into those black waters, the ship beneath one's feet tilting and sinking, very often meant that there were only minutes left. The human frame could not long withstand the freezing shock. And with each vast consignment of wheat or grain that was sent to the seabed, the nation's chances of defeating Nazism were diminished.

For the convoys to sail as safely as possible from these predations, they needed a constant stream of acute intelligence, giving them co-ordinates and freshly confounding new routes to swerve would-be attackers. The armed naval vessels in the convoys also needed to be pointed towards potential attackers, so that counter-attacks could be launched. Given that this theatre of war spanned the whole vastness of the North Atlantic Ocean, the prospect was daunting and fearful. But very swiftly a brilliant co-ordinating control base was established, first in the south-coast port of Plymouth, but then, just months into the war, relocated to the mighty port city of Liverpool in the north-west of the country.

This was where thousands of ships in convoys were arriving with their invaluable cargoes and where they were being repaired and refitted before being sent out into the northern darkness of those seas once more. The people of Liverpool were already throwing themselves with vigour into the war effort, and they were now a target for the relentless Luftwaffe. The port and the residential city were bombed with terrible ferocity over and over again.

Nerve centre: main control room of the Western Approaches
underground war rooms in Liverpool – now a wonderful museum.

The new base that would control and guide the Convoys had to be established in a thoroughly secure location. The answer was a government building called Derby House, and a secretly excavated underground complex of some 100 rooms, dominated by an extraordinary, vast and still beautifully preserved central control room.

Across one wall of this mighty chamber (the ceiling was about thirty feet high) was a huge and intensely detailed map of the Atlantic in rich dark blue, where Wrens plotted the positions of convoys and enemy submarines partly by climbing up on tall moveable ladders. Rather like Bletchley Park, all three services – the Navy, Air Force and Army – were making their contributions in this glitteringly modern chamber, furnished with map tables and galleries above with telephones and telexes and Type-X encryption machines, for the scrambling of messages to keep them beyond enemy intelligence. There was another room in which signals received, also in code, could be run through the necessary decoding technology. Much intelligence was being gathered in via air reconnaissance. The secrecy was, naturally, intense and the minute any new recruit walked over the threshold, they were required to sign the Official Secrets Act, and the secrecy had no time limit placed upon it. Many assumed that it was for life. Staff came to know the underground base as 'the dungeon'. But it was much brighter and more exciting than the nickname implied. The official title was 'Western Approaches Command', and its originating genius was Commander Gilbert Roberts who – even though relatively young at forty – had previously been invalided out of the Navy after suffering tuberculosis. He was thrilled to be thrown into the centre of the war's vortex.

Here, beneath the streets of Liverpool, and under conditions of confidentiality that were actually intended to last fifty years, life-and-death manoeuvres were plotted by Wrens. It was like a huge game of Battleships on a giant grid on the floor. One such strategy was known as 'Raspberry' and it had arisen out of a mystery: was it possible that Nazi submarines were not simply approaching convoys – and then opening fire – but actually sailing with them, invisibly? That is, were the U-boats mirroring the convoys' courses underwater? Captain Roberts and several Wrens plotted out a range of possible scenarios. Working through the night, they calculated angles and depths; and the answer was yes. The submarines which formed so-called 'wolf packs' attached themselves to the rears of convoys, where look-outs were less likely, and then submerged to positions directly below hulls. But the team at Western Approaches understood that in such positions, U-boats could be very swiftly detected by the ships above and if a vessel was targeted, the naval escorts could swiftly sweep the area and drop depth charges, hitting the attacker before it could either deliver more carnage, or make its escape. The term 'raspberry' arose because each time a depth charge hit its U-boat target, this was what was being 'blown' towards the Nazis. Other strategies carried similarly themed fruit and vegetable names, from 'Artichoke' to 'Gooseberry'. Light-heartedness was scarce in this theatre of war, and in this subterranean base, each naval operative had no difficulty envisaging what the crews in the wild Atlantic storms were facing.

The base also played host to the 'Western Approaches Tactical Unit'. Raw intelligence was fine as far as it went but captains and commanders of vessels also had to be taught about U-boat tactics, and the sort of thinking that *their* captains did. This was the real value of codebreaking espionage: not just gaining ideas of positions, but also developing deep insights into the strategic thinking of the enemy and the means of attack that they most favoured.

Yet while the atmosphere at Western Approaches was focused and serious and fast, innocent escapism was seen as a valuable pressure valve. And so, in the winter of 1944, the team in the base succeeded in staging an ambitious pantomime production of *Aladdin*. There were naval ratings in drag and others dressed in false beards, robes and turbans. One of the show's leading luminaries was Wren June Duncan, an accomplished dancer and budding actress and model, who had been assigned to Western Approaches aged just seventeen. Her work at the base required lightning-fast mental agility, with a special talent for mental arithmetic. And while June Duncan's post-war career was a swirl of 1950s sophistication, modelling for *Tatler* and *Vogue*, travelling to Paris to appear in haute couture fashion shows for Christian Dior, nothing could dim her achievement in contributing with such skill to the most vital of war duties. In later years, she wrote: 'Sometimes I look at myself in the mirror and wonder if I dreamed those heady days at the peak of my career in the glamour and fashion world.' Yet her career in the naval world had been another peak, this one like a secret dream. The work that she and her naval colleagues did that involved fast-moving real-time updates from convoys in the Atlantic, being plotted with intense precision and anticipating as far as possible the lurking hazard of U-boats, was directly instrumental in both Britain's survival and in its eventual victory.

And her time at Western Approaches made this dancer light on her feet in other ways. At one stage, there was one young naval officer posted to Liverpool in order to absorb the full range of the intelligence and strategy-making. Strikingly, every Wren was under orders never to make eye contact with this man. He was the young Prince Philip. Naturally, June Duncan *did* catch his eye, in the sort of situation that has been played out in a thousand romantic comedies; she was teetering uncertainly along the corridor carrying a tall pile of books and related papers. The inevitable crash, fall and chaos ensued and as the young prince jumped forward to help Wren Duncan gather all the material from the floor, gazes could not help but be met. Even that miniature transgression earned Wren Duncan the stern disapproval of her superiors. But it was an episode of absurd innocence in a time of intense severity.

HOW TO GET THERE

After many decades when the bunker stayed wreathed in shadow, Western Approaches is now a fascinating museum, restored in all details to its 1945 condition, from the vast rich blue wall with its Atlantic plotting grid, to all the desks with their Bakelite telephones. The address is 1–3 Rumford Street, not far from Albert Dock. The nearest metro station is Moorfields.

The Cavern and the Hill

Bentley Priory, near Stanmore, Middlesex

The clocks were a small touch of genius; they might even now be described as design classics. Throughout the Battle of Britain, however, they were vital. In an underground Operations Room among a symphony of brass and wood and bright light, dominated by a vast table bearing a map of Europe and innumerable brightly coloured counters, the clock was a clever reference point. There were two concentric rings on the face, the outer displaying the hours one to twelve, the inner showing the numbers of the twenty-four-hour clock. Between each hour were alternating triangles of colour: yellow, blue, red. These were to enable WAAFs to update, with the swiftest of glances, in every fifteen-minute period, the similarly coloured counters that they were working with on the map tables. This was the only concession to simplicity in the entire secret operation. These were women and men whose interior mental landscapes were governed by complex trigonometrical calculations. How the women in this underground complex found the time to invent a wholly fictional – and sex-mad – WAAF called

*Tight plotting: Operations Room at RAF Fighter Command
at Bentley Priory near Watford.*

Lottie Crump to tease their male colleagues with was a
mystery in itself.

In terms of RAF Fighter Command, and the nerve
centre of that lethal summer of 1940, when the Luftwaffe
and the possibilities of Nazi invasion were being held off
by preternaturally brave young men in Spitfires, the public
is probably now more familiar with the 11 Group Operations Room in Uxbridge. Based on the western fringe of
London, this was where Sir Keith Park presided over the
battle that was determining the nation's future. The large
table with maps and moveable plaques, the WAAFs like
croupiers, the high ceiling, the telephones, the wall of

squadron-by-squadron indicators, the green-shaded lights and the balcony above are also familiar from an entire sub-genre of war films. Yet just a few miles to the north-east, an even grander – and even more secret – prospect had been hewn out of the earth in early 1940 just before the onslaught.

Bentley Priory was (and is) a wonderfully elegant surprise in the woods a few miles to the south of Watford. A magnificent eighteenth-century house, largely rebuilt and reimagined by Sir John Soane, with an Italianate bell tower, was in one sense an incongruously beautiful setting for the lightning-paced practicalities of the modern RAF. It was also, in its historic social heyday, visited by Prime Ministers Pitt, Canning and Liverpool, and poets and writers such as William Wordsworth and Sir Walter Scott. But it had huge advantages. It was fifteen miles from the centre of London, close enough for all matters of political urgency but sufficiently far away and secluded to evade the attentions of mass bombers and in addition to this, its hilltop position gave the on-site personnel the startling and sometimes terrifying view of the London Blitz below with the distant sky burning orange and bright ruby. All who worked here could see directly how intensely vital their roles were.

The property had been acquired by the RAF in 1936. As with many grand country properties, there were dwindling numbers of people who could actually afford to own and maintain them. The house had been a hotel, and then a girls' boarding school. The RAF picked it up on reasonable terms. Air Chief Marshal Hugh Dowding was the man in charge of Fighter Command. He was a restrained and slightly melancholic figure, who felt very deeply when it came to the lives of his young airmen, and he attended seances in the hope of contacting those who had fallen. He was also sharply analytical, and it was at Bentley Priory that the 'Dowding System' first came into operation. In essence, at a time when radar and all of its possibilities were completely new, this was a nationwide chain of communication that would feed information about incoming enemy aircraft back to a central control room that had been dug beneath the grounds of the big house. The intelligence would be collated, positions and courses calculated and plotted, and the young airmen of Fighter Command would be launched into the air to meet

The view from on high: the eighteenth-century beauty of Bentley Priory.

the incoming threats, accurately, with correct co-ordinates and smooth timing.

Theirs was the heroism, but the secret work involved in analysing and relaying the information they needed was exacting in its own way. The bunker at Bentley Priory in fact had two nerve centres: the Filter Room, into which all the raw intelligence from bases around the country flowed, and the Operations Room, which then received the pure distillation of all that information. Both were daunting prospects in terms of mental endurance. In the earliest days, recalled Eileen Younghusband, there had been a number of stockbrokers recruited from the City as they were supposed to be able to handle mathematical data at tremendous speeds. But it also transpired that there was a reservoir of female talent in this area and the young women recruited to the Women's Air Force sat a dazzling range of proficiency tests. Younghusband herself had been an all-rounder at school; she was not just acute on mathematics, but poly-lingual too. She also had fantastic initiative and at only sixteen, she had taken herself to France to make a living as an au pair without any introductions or contacts. It was only the looming storms of war that brought her back, and into the productive work in the Filter Room. Meanwhile, teenager Gladys Eva, who had not excelled on paper at school, was a whizz at bridge and other complex card games, which was enough to demonstrate that she could not only hold complicated formulas in her head, but also keep relatively calm under intense pressure. The same was true of young journalist

Patricia Clark, who didn't especially like her destined career trajectory of editing *Woman and Beauty* magazine. She joined up and again, lightning quick-wittedness plus a certain coolness marked her out as ideal.

And these young women were brilliantly matched with the young boffins and technicians, who they teased terribly. The legend of Lottie Crump began as a brilliant chain joke when young women officers like Eileen Young-husband would come on to shift with female colleagues talking loudly about the scandalous exploits of their newest recruit, an imaginary blonde society beauty. Achingly, the young men began to ask when they were going to see Lottie Crump on shift. The reasons for her continual absence became ever sexier and more surreal; on one occasion, there had been an accident involving stockings and on another, Lottie had done herself an injury in the bath 'while playing with toy boats'. That said, the young air officers could be equally boisterous with their female colleagues. Any young lady entering the next-door Bentley Officers Mess for the first time was required by tradition to remove her shoes, dab her feet in the ash of a spent fire, then be hoisted up and turned upside down so that she might leave her footprints on the ceiling.

At the deadliest of times, with young pilots required to summon almost unimaginable courage, and with London crackling with flames, such energetic good humour was vital. There were many RAF control bases around the country, such as the establishment down at Rudloe Manor in Wiltshire. But Bentley Priory somehow came to reflect the grave and benevolent soul of Sir Hugh Dowding. Internal politics pole-axed his career not long after victory in the Battle of Britain when his strategies were deemed insufficiently barnstorming and aggressive. Happily, he is held in warmer memory now. And while the 11 Group Bunker at Uxbridge is now a brilliant museum dedicated to the Battle of Britain, Bentley Priory, which is also now a museum, has a slightly wider remit. It takes in the story of the Royal Observation Corps, who were the men and women who gave early warnings of incoming attacks, and who could identify all the different types of enemy craft almost just by their engine noise. It also features a haunting tribute to the Air Chief Marshal who believed in the literal truth of angels.

How to get there

Bentley Priory museum is worth visiting not just for the history and the rather brilliant reconstructions of the Filter and Operations Rooms, plus Dowding's office, and some beguiling interactive gimmicks, but also for the prospect of enjoying some lovely architecture and nice views in attractively landscaped grounds. Bentley Priory estate lies between Stanmore and Watford, on Common Road. To get there via public transport, take the Jubilee Line to its terminus at Stanmore, and from outside the station it is a ten-minute journey on the 142 bus. Equally, you could get the Bakerloo Line or London Overground to Harrow and Wealdstone, and from there catch a 258 bus to Common Road.

SECRET VILLAGES

The Village that Stopped

Tyneham, Dorset

The lush green wooded slope, with emerald grass growing from pale chalk, gently runs down to a tranquil sea. This place stands apart from the wider world and even, in a way, from time itself. There are ruins here, but unlike the great wrecks of abbeys, or medieval fortresses, these fragments of stone have a melancholic intimacy. Here was a row of tiny cottages and over there was a post office. A little further up the hill, stood the big rectory and a grand house. The church still stands, though there has been no one to worship there for a very long time. Towards the latter end of the war, this village, tucked deep in the verdant folds of Dorset, and lying just yards away from a once-busy fishing community at Worbarrow Bay, suddenly ceased to exist. Its echo was still there on old maps, its name plain enough to see, but in the winter of 1943, that name was erased. Even to approach it on foot was a civil offence. The families who had lived in the village's tiny cottages yearned for the day that they could at last return to old familiar surroundings. That day never came. The village was, and is, called Tyneham.

And even though the veil of obscurity has been lifted, and day-tripping visitors are allowed to explore it at certain set times, its story still carries a resonant note of sadness. Most of us can recognise the anguish of being torn from a loved home.

Yet in the winter of 1943, Tyneham was needed. The complex and ambitious plans for D-Day were being formulated and the army needed secluded locations, far from the unfriendly eyes of any possible agents, where weaponry might be tested. This corner of Dorset was already active in tank practice: the nearby Lulworth Ranges had been in use for this purpose since the end of the First World War. But in an age of fast-modernising materiel, an expansion was necessary. And the War Office did not consider the land-grab too much of a loss. In terms of population, Tyneham was perhaps more of a hamlet than a village, a quaint prospect of thatched roofs, a little church and muddy roads. Indeed, even by 1943, it could have been walked through by any of Thomas Hardy's rural protagonists and none of them would have looked out of place. In the depths of war, there was no room for sentiment, and it was decided that the people living in the hamlet would have to be found alternative accommodation in nearby towns. Yet despite all of this, there was a speed and a ruthlessness to the evacuation which haunts the imagination to this day.

The 225 villagers received official communication from the government in December 1943 and they had a month to gather their possessions and prepare themselves for evacuation. There were families who had lived there for generations and so the shock was intense. The government letter was breezy in its insistence that they accept their fate: 'The government appreciate that this is no small sacrifice which you are asked to make,' ran the letter, 'but they are sure that you will give this further help towards winning the war with a good heart.'[32]

The unintended cruelty was that the villagers were led to believe that once the war was finally won, they would be allowed to return from temporary exile. Yet in the sharp air of the Cold War that immediately followed victory in Europe, this aspiration was soon smothered by the government. The land and the village were still needed, this time for even more secret manoeuvres, in case war should come again.

The land, and the village, with all its houses, was owned by the Bond family. To describe the way of life in 1943 as traditional would be a grave understatement. The villagers were all tied tenants and the area was enfolded in centuries of history that to outsiders might have felt a shade medieval. The Bond family itself was not protected from this government incursion though. Interviewed a few years ago, Major-General Mark Bond, whose father was, to use the common term, lord of the manor, recalled when he returned to Britain from the war in 1945 and his father met him at the nearby railway station at Wareham. 'My father greeted me,' said Major-General Bond, 'and I remember being in the car when he told me, "we're living in Corfe Castle".'[33]

As billets go, there were worse. 'He understood with the war coming to its climax, it was absolutely necessary to give tanks the proper training area,' added Major General Bond. But others have observed too that in a sense, the villagers were already well used to the idea of their lives being rigidly controlled; as tied tenants, their labours were in essence for the manor. Before it was evacuated, by 1943, the village was already living in a form of twilight. The modern world had moved away with speed with main roads and motor cars passing by Tyneham, and jobs and the village's young people moving away too, even from the fishing concerns down at nearby Worbarrow Bay. There were fewer and fewer pupils for the little village school. Tyneham might have been idyllic and rustic but fewer and fewer people knew that it was there. So, the decision simply to keep it as a semi-secret army training ground was in some ways quite easy, otherwise why use taxpayer's money to prop up a tiny dwindling community that could not fund its own services?

Yet the wartime government and all its successors equally could not quite understand the poetry and the ache of loss, or the sense that many villagers felt that they had been arbitrarily expelled from their own Eden. That agonised yearning to return persisted for decades, even as the small houses with their increasingly bare thatched roofs became more and more dilapidated. In 1974, Tyneham villager John Gould wrote a pleading letter to the then Prime Minister Harold Wilson. 'Tyneham to me is the most beautiful place in the world,' he wrote, 'and I

The silent village: after Tyneham was evacuated, none were permitted to walk its streets.

want to give the rest of my life and energy to its restoration . . . most of all, I want to go home.'[34] Those final five words are in some ways among the most powerful in the language. But that home, that Eden, was already long lost. The way of life in Tyneham was extinct, agriculture was now mechanised and fishing the work of trawlers from big harbours. And by then, the cottages were literal ruins – roofless, open to the stormy sky. The rectory and the big house were hollowed out and crumbling.

As with all ruins, though, the very idea of Tyneham in more recent years has evoked a different sort of yearning among outsiders. The appetite to see the village that disappeared into the Secrets Act was sharpening. Poignantly, for that villager John Gould, the Ministry of Defence yielded a fraction a year after his complaint, though not for residential purposes. In 1975, certain footpaths were opened up again for very restricted hours and only upon certain days of the year. As well as the skeletal decay of the cottages, everyone returning would have seen that the Elizabethan manor house had vanished as unfortunately it had been demolished by the authorities in 1967.

But even though the land was – and still is, to this day – used for military training purposes, the authorities gradually began to find ways to allow eager tourists from farther afield to explore what had become a tremendous mystery. Now, access is rather more generous, and the village and the nearby stretch of coastline are very popular with great numbers of people.

Major-General Bond's own links with the village occasioned sharp pangs of nostalgia. When he was interviewed some years ago, he said, 'It has its old magic and a rather sorrowful background. I'm sad that what I knew of the people and the village no longer exists and the houses are in ruins.'[35] Yet perhaps in another sense, the secrecy of war paradoxically both destroyed Tyneham and preserved it. For unlike the tourist-village honeypots of the Cotswolds with streams of coach parties and themed tea shops, Tyneham was arrested in a particular moment of time, and it has frozen with a quality of silence, reflection and melancholy.

How to get there

Tyneham lies just off the B3070, close to Lulworth, and is not far from the town of Swanage. The area and the village are signposted. The nearest railway station is Wareham. The permitted hours for visiting are still quite strict and there are days when the area will not be accessible at all so make sure you seek out the most up-to-date information on the site before visiting.

The Village and the Distant Dead

Imber, Wiltshire

It remains in some ways a prehistoric landscape, denuded of its farming and of its working population. The hills and the hollows have folded back into the forms that they held thousands of years ago when Neolithic men just a few miles east were erecting those vast blue-grey stones in concentric circles. The turf is still ridged with unfathomably old burial sites. On top of this, nature has asserted itself in ways not possible in other more cultivated parts of the country. Here are rare juniper, exquisite orchids, dancing marsh fritillary butterflies and a vast expanse of dry grassland on chalk, thought to be among the largest in western Europe. But this region also contains the ghost of a village that vanished from the public realm and became the shadow of a secret, like Tyneham, in 1943. The village was, and is, called Imber. Yet unlike Tyneham, life continued, in a radically different form. The village's simulacrum survived in the same spot and where once agricultural workers lived and laboured, now soldiers ran down the lanes between the houses, bellowing and firing weapons. The village had been resurrected, but for the purposes of teaching the armed forces about street fighting and about combating enemy soldiers and terrorists in built-up environments. All of which seems amazingly at odds with the rich timelessness of the land all around.

Imber lies almost directly in the centre of Salisbury Plain. It was always a fair distance from any of the nearest market towns to the east or west or north. It had always been noted for that sense of apartness. The first recorded settlement first appeared on that wind-whistling plain during the tenth century and it earned itself a mention in the following century's Domesday Book, as the Norman invaders took stock of their freshly seized riches. The village evolved throughout the centuries – the church established at the start went through various incarnations of stone and the version that survives to this day still carries traces of the thirteenth century – but the way of life remained stolidly quiet. By the late nineteenth century, the main village street was a prospect of heavily thatched cottages, an inn and the manor house close by, all dominated by the church which lay at the top of a slight incline. By the 1930s, with the world beyond buzzing with neon, the skies droning with aeroplanes, and the winding country roads elsewhere honking with new middle-class motorists, Imber still retained its nineteenth-century identity. The farming equipment, intended for the local crops of wheat and oats was not very far in advance of that featured in *Far from the Madding Crowd*, and the extravagantly thatched cottages with straw roofs almost completely swaddling the dwellings beneath remained free of the swanky modern conveniences of ice boxes, hot water and flushing lavatories.

But the people of Imber were aware for many years of the extremely unusual position they occupied. Since the late nineteenth century, Salisbury Plain had been used by the military for a variety of training purposes. Acre by acre, the amount of ground that the army laid claim to was steadily increasing. What had begun as simply taking a small corner of the Plain was becoming spreading encroachment. The First World War and its neurotic aftermath set the destiny of the Plain and the village. Imber by now was surrounded by firing ranges and the air frequently echoed with the roar of approaching tanks. The army had been buying up all the land surrounding the village (some of which was in the gift of the Earl of Longleat) so that by 1943, Imber was wholly encircled.

Its fate had not always been clear cut. In fact, by the early 1930s there had been a historic shift within the village bounds. The local authorities had built some brand new council houses, anticipating a time when new families might want to move there, and when the village might take some steps closer to the modern age. The demands of 1943 meant that that day never came. As with the people of Tyneham, the residents of Imber – all of whom were rent-paying tenants – received their eviction notices. The US Army needed the wider area, and the village itself, for vital training before the invasion of Europe. Those who had lived in Imber all their lives received forty-seven days' notice to pack up and leave. Alternative accommodation was sought in nearby towns like Warminster. The people of Imber were left with the powerful impression that the move would be purely temporary. When peace had come to Europe, they would be able to return home and resume their old lives. The authorities had different ideas.

In 1943, and in the years after the war, the village simply vanished from the map. It was as though it had never existed. Those who had lived there now had to face the prospect that they were lost to their old homes for ever. They could not even visit fleetingly because all the roads leading to Imber were blocked to general traffic. None could pass, even on foot. The government had simply decided that the territory was too valuable to the military, in terms of preparing for all the conflicts to come. So, while the residents were forced to shrug and accept their new lives, their old village street was put to extraordinarily lively and deadly use.

The only building to survive was St Giles's Church. Its historic treasures were redistributed to other dioceses, but some fourteenth- and fifteenth-century wall paintings remained. A renovated version of the village's pub, the Bell Inn, also stood steadfast. But the cottages and the tiny houses were not really ideal for the purposes of conveying a tough urban environment for soldiers to carefully pick their way through. In the years after the war, these were to be replaced with new blocks that were mock-ups of houses and apartment buildings. It was said that by the early 1970s, these were being put to sombre use as a simulacrum of the streets of Northern Ireland, with the troops being trained in combating dissident armed Republicans. The honeyed air of Salisbury Plain was in some ways a poor substitute for the iron-skied Belfast.

In general terms, during the war years, the government did try to ensure that those who were displaced or who had their homes acquired for a variety of army purposes, were fairly compensated. But the sadness of Imber for those nostalgic for it was the sudden impenetrable layer of secrecy that fell over the place. None were to know what was happening there, and none were to know what had become of beloved cottages, and the prospects of the high street. Memories were dissolving and could not be prompted by visits to familiar spots. Nostalgia was one thing, but the knowledge that all traces of earlier life had now been swept away prompted a darker melancholia.

There were later incursions though, and in 1961, a small band campaigning for the restoration of Imber led by a man called Austin Underwood, did manage somehow to reach the village and declaim their speeches from outside the Grade 1 listed church. Added to this, there were eventually compassionate occasions when former villagers were allowed to visit the untouched graveyard to tend to the plots of their relatives. It was also in 1961 that the question of perhaps allowing the village to resume its former life was raised in Parliament and Whitehall. But the answer was a firm no. Now, almost eighty years on, one of the results is that the secret village has now become something of a forbidden temptation to masses of country ramblers and rural explorers. If you walk now on the

The echo of the past: the evacuated village of Imber kept its grip on the hearts of those who had lived there.

fringes of the military border of Salisbury Plain, itself a thrilling and pleasing landscape of Bronze Age hill fortifications, with the occasional distant prospect of burnt-out tanks, the discreet yet firm nature of that borderline is made plain by relaxed, good-humoured soldiers who tell you politely but implacably that you cannot continue along certain paths. The reasoning, after all, is benign: live ammunition is being fired. Would you really want to be shot in the head for the sake of seeing some grassland?

But there are open days now too, once super-rare glints in the calendar, now becoming more frequent. On these days the Ministry of Defence relents and visitors in motor transport are allowed to stream through. In recent years, there have been convoys of bright red Routemaster buses, underlining a certain eccentricity in the insistence upon being allowed to roam across this forbidden plain. Tea is served in the church. Other than that, the mocked-up buildings are not much to look at – that is, if you have no links to the village. Conversely, for relatives of families who lived there, these days are rare opportunities to at least take in the landscape that shaped their loved ones. And perhaps, unlike a great many city streets upon which houses fall and flats rise in a steady cycle of gentrification or decay, making entire districts unrecognisable from one generation to the next, the contours of the hills and hollows around Imber are paradoxically preserved rather beautifully. This is a secret corner of the country that even Neolithic man would recognise today.

How to get there

The best guides to when the village might once more be accessible can be found through visitwiltshire.com and the Ministry of Defence website. A direct road to Imber climbs out of Warminster, about six miles to the west. Warminster is on the A350 and the A36 and can also be reached by rail, with regular services to Bristol and Salisbury. Even on summery days when Imber is closed off, there are some hugely satisfying walks that can be taken around these fringes of Salisbury Plain, to get a sense of both the richness and the strangeness of the landscape that is characterised by Bronze Age earthworks in juxtaposition with distant concrete blast walls. The paths are clearly signposted to prevent any chance of you wandering into live shelling and being blown to smithereens.

Conclusion

There is something about each of the different secret landscapes and houses and tunnels of Britain that imparts a strong flavour of what it was like to live through the war. In amid all the ubiquitous imagery of old black and white films, with a million upper lips resolute in their stiffness, the once-secret sites give a rather more colourful and more nuanced insight. Just as the towering achievements at Bletchley Park were not just boffins and mad machinery – instead, this was a quasi-university at which young women and men from all walks of life lived, learned and frequently fell in love – there were also so many other classified locations that told stories of unpredictable humanity.

And those realms held out so many new possibilities for young women who, before the war, would have been looking at the prospect of shop or factory work, followed by marriage and children and housekeeping. Whether based in the secret listening HQs at Scarborough or Forest Moor or working in the secret tunnels near Birmingham and Mold or out on the rocket site at Borth, the darkness of the war meant that at last their talents and capabilities could be expressed in wholly new ways. Though as some of Bletchley's distinguished veterans like Sheila Lawn and Jean Valentine observed, the years that followed the war proved a sharp and disappointing readjustment, as women were expected to return to their old lives.

Some of those secret locations also demonstrate the breathtaking scope of the wartime imagination. The cathedral-like oil storage tunnels at Easter Ross for instance were almost Victorian in their ambition. They were also almost Victorian when it came to the workforce and it is instructive to see that even as late as the 1930s, a largely imported Irish workforce was being sent to work in gruelling conditions that the nineteenth-century railway navvies would have recognised. And elsewhere there were questions of sharp class discrimination, seen in the laboratories of Dollis Hill where the wild talent of East End-born Tommy Flowers was glaringly obvious once this engineering genius was given the opportunity to exercise it, summoning a programmable computer into physical existence for the very first time. And yet there were those who only heard his accent and saw only his lack of Oxford or Cambridge certificates, and instantly dismissed out of hand anything that he had to say.

The secret locations also tell a sombre story about illimitable human courage. The women and men who were trained as SOE agents on those private Scottish estates, being taught the art of death in deep hidden glens, knew that there was every chance that they were also being taught to face their own deaths. The prospect of being parachuted deep into enemy territory, with no friends or allies, and no possibility of back-up or rescue, must have given dread the weight of lead. Yet somehow they managed to absorb this fear into their beings and never let it erode their determination. The stark beauty of those training grounds tells its own story of survival: such harsh landscapes themselves have no comfort to offer spies or fugitives.

And the wider hidden history of the country, from the bombed streets put to use as training grounds to the slightly obscure Victorian country mansions being turned into intelligence nerve centres, from the tube tunnels used as arms factories to the wildernesses used to help engineer rockets, peels back unexpected layers in landscapes that might once have seemed familiar. Throughout those years of war, it was not only the people who were co-opted en masse into the struggle – so too were mist-enshrouded Suffolk shingle beaches, lonely west country moors and the dark earth beneath the forest floors. In some cases, the sites have a sombreness as they focus the mind on the innumerable sacrifices made. But in other instances, the secret history adds an extra flourish of delight, as with Blenheim Palace, which is an extraordinarily rich spectacle on its own account, but whose overwhelming pomp is seasoned fantastically with the knowledge that some of Britain's snobbier social-climbing spies prowled around the premises, yearning to meet and be accepted by the aristocracy.

Then there are the locations, such as the windswept hills outside Scarborough, where the secrecy continues, commendably, today. The defence of the realm is still vital, and there are still women and men signing the Official

Secrets Act and going about their hidden work with intense diligence.

Indeed, the secret history also tells us that there was a period, long before Instagram and Twitter, when the British were world-beaters in the art of discretion. The truth was that the injunction to beware 'careless talk' was obeyed meticulously because fundamentally these confidential sites and projects were thrilling posts and to be in on such classified work was itself frequently considered an immense privilege. Some time ago, the ultra-silent former codebreakers of Bletchley Park, who were at last at liberty to discuss their amazing wartime roles after decades in the shadows, were asked if such secrecy would be at all possible in the modern age. Some burst out laughing at the very idea, yet for the very few who have had the chance to visit a certain modern doughnut-shaped headquarters in Cheltenham – GCHQ, the spiritual descendant of Bletchley Park – that quality of keeping lips buttoned actually does remain today.

Above all, the terrain of Secret Britain tells a story of the most astounding creativity and ingenuity, frequently seasoned with intense good humour and affection. And even the saddest stories, such as the lost villages, now, at this distance, carry with them an agreeable air of elegiac melancholy which also seems an integral part of many of the UK's ancient landscapes.

In the years when national character was shaped by war, all the secret properties, estates and terrains fundamentally spoke also of optimism, and the belief that even the most terrible enemies could be vanquished.

Acknowledgements

Over the years, I have been privileged to meet and interview some wonderful people who played integral roles in the landscape of Secret Britain, and – among them – I would like to take the opportunity to once more thank Chris Barnes, Ray Fautley and the much-missed Jean Valentine for some unforgettable insights into a vanished world. At Headline, my deep gratitude to Sarah Emsley for embracing the entire idea with such enthusiasm, and to Katie Packer who has, throughout trying times, worked with real ingenuity and creativity to bring this book into being. It benefited illimitably from the laser-beam eyes of copyeditor Natasha Onwuemezi and proofreader Jill Cole. Imbuing the book with heart and atmosphere are the haunting and evocative illustrations by artist Helen Cann, plus Cathie Arrington and her superb picture research. I'm also very grateful to the ceaselessly energetic Jessica Farrugia for incisive publicity, ensuring word of this once-secret land is spread. Many thanks to history enthusiast Louise Hayman who read through the manuscript to give legal advice. Huge gratitude also to my brilliant agent Anna Power who has been endlessly encouraging throughout.

PICTURE CREDITS

Endnotes

1) It was after the Nazis shockingly swept through France in June 1940 that Churchill appointed the Labour politician (and Chancellor-to-be) Hugh Dalton to set up the Special Operations Executive with its mission to 'set Europe ablaze', as Dalton recalled in his diary.

2) Vera Atkins, quoted in an interview with Madeleine Masson for Masson's 1975 book *Christine* (Virago, 2005).

3) Heydrich accrued many sinister nicknames throughout his vile career; these included 'the blond beast' and 'the hangman'. The 'Butcher' nickname originated in Czechoslovakia, where he presided over a nightmare regime of death and torture.

4) Margaret Herterich wrote a wonderfully evocative account of her time in Ynyslas, which can be found in the Imperial War Museum Collections, document number 99/86/1.

5) As quoted in *The Secret Listeners* (Aurum Press, 2012), by the author.

6) As quoted on a terrific page of the North Devon Areas of Outstanding Natural Beauty website and including some archive footage of US troops on those beaches, plus striking images of the PLUTO project. www.northdevon-aonb.org.uk/coastalheritage/world-war-2/d-day.

7) For more news of the accessibility of the area around MOD Shoeburyness, visit www.qinetiq.com/en/shoeburyness.

8) As quoted in the *York Press*, 18 March 2019, and also on a lovely website called www.herstoryyork.org.uk.

9) Florence Clark was interviewed for a succulent book called *The Sweethearts* by Lynn Russell and Neil Hanson (HarperCollins, 2013).

10) *York Press*, 18 March 2019.

11) Ray Fautley, interviewed by the author in 2011.

12) Jean Valentine, interviewed many times by the author! (I am proud to say that she was a good – and deeply inspirational – friend.)

13) As above.

14) As remembered by Mimi Galilee (another wonderful friend), interviewed by the author. Mimi also stayed on at the base for a short while after the war at the point when RAF Eastcote was about to regenerate into GCHQ.

15) Ivy Kenworthy, as quoted in *Breaking Teleprinter Ciphers at Bletchley Park*, an edition of a once-secret official report written in 1945 and declassified fifty-five years later (Wiley IEEE Press, 2015).

16) Michael Loewe contributed a fascinating essay to the pioneering 1993 book *Codebreakers: The Inside Story of Bletchley Park* (OUP).

17) There is a lovely interview with Margaret O'Connell and several of her former Bletchley colleagues where they discuss not only the intense and fraught nature of the work, but also the food at wartime Woburn, which featured, as Betty Warwick recalled, 'fish with maggots in it'. Go to www.bbc.co.uk/news/technology-27294569.

18) For the full story of Constance Babington Smith and RAF Medmenham, Taylor Downing's *Spies in the Sky: The Secret Battle for Ariel Intelligence in World War II* (Abacus, 2012) is illuminating and engaging.

19) Chris Barnes, as interviewed by the author in 2011.

20) As quoted in *The Secret Listeners* (2012) by the author.

21) Rene Pederson, as above.

22) As quoted in *The Secret Listeners*, as above.

23) Joan Nicholls wrote a memoir entitled *England Needs You: The Story of Beaumanor Y Station* (Joan Nicholls, 2000).

24) As quoted in *Winston Churchill's Toyshop: The Inside Story of Military Intelligence* by Stuart Macrae (Amberley Publishing, 2012).

25) After those hair-raising boyhood scrapes, Gordon Rogers became an eminently respectable chartered surveyor and keen military historian and astronomer, who was interviewed for a 2015 Discovery Channel documentary – *Churchill's Toyshop* – and whose public talks about 'Churchill's Toyshop' (and his own escapades) have been very popular.

26) Sarah Baring, as interviewed by the author in 2009.

27) Mimi Galillee, as interviewed by the author in 2009.

28) As interviewed by BBC Scotland in September 2019. For more quotes, and some exceptionally eerie photographs, go to www.bbc.co.uk/news/uk-scotland-highlands-islands-49728273.

29) Local historian Colin Barber has done a brilliant and atmospheric job of investigating the hidden history of the tunnels, and much information can be found at www.rhydymwynvalleyhistory.co.uk.

30) As quoted (among other places) on an interesting BBC Wales report on the operation. Go to www.bbc.co.uk/news/uk-wales-48308512.

31) As quoted in a fascinating *Daily Mail* article from 2015, which can be found here: www.dailymail.co.uk/news/article-3053771/Wartime-scientist-91-revisits-secret-underground-factory-helped-build-Lancaster-engines-safe-Hitler-s-bombs.html.

32) Some fascinating archival material and interviews – including newspaper interviews with Brigadier Mark Bond – are now becoming available online at Mark Bond Archives | Tyneham (tynehamopc.org.uk).

33) As above.

34) This heartbreaking open letter was written to Harold Wilson in 1974, and as well as being quoted by newspapers, it later inspired a theatre company to make a visit to the village.

35) Interviewed by the BBC in October 2013.